Kittlitz's and Marbled Murrelets in Kenai Fjords National Park, South-Central Alaska: At-Sea Distribution, Abundance, and Foraging Habitat, 2006–08

By M.L. Arimitsu, J.F. Piatt, M.D. Romano, E.N. Madison, and J.S. Conaway

Prepared in cooperation with Kenai Fjords National Park

Open-File Report 2010-1181

U.S. Department of the Interior
U.S. Geological Survey

U.S. Department of the Interior
KEN SALAZAR, Secretary

U.S. Geological Survey
Marcia K. McNutt, Director

U.S. Geological Survey, Reston, Virginia: 2010

For more information on the USGS—the Federal source for science about the Earth, its natural and living resources, natural hazards, and the environment, visit *http://www.usgs.gov* or call 1-888-ASK-USGS

For an overview of USGS information products, including maps, imagery, and publications, visit *http://ww.usgs.gov/pubprod*

To order this and other USGS information products, visit http://store.usgs.gov

Suggested citation:
Arimitsu, M.L., Piatt, J.F., Romano, M.D., Madison, E.N., and Conaway, J.S., 2010, Kittlitz's and Marbled Murrelets in Kenai Fjords National Park, south-central Alaska: At-sea distribution, abundance, and foraging habitat, 2006–08: U.S. Geological Survey Open-File Report 2010-1181, 68 p.

Contents

Figures

Tables

Conversion Factors, and Abbreviations, Acronyms, and Symbols

Conversion Factors

SI units to Inch-Pound

Multiply	By	To obtain
millimeter (mm)	0.03937	inch (in.)
kilometer (km)	0.6214	mile (mi)
meter (m)	3.281	foot (ft)
square kilometer (km^2)	0.3861	square mile (mi^2)
square meter (m^2)	10.76	square foot (ft^2)
gram (g)	0.03527	ounce, avoirdupois (oz)
cubic meter per second (m^3/s)	35.31	cubic foot per second (ft^3/s)
meter per second (m/s)	3.281	foot per second (ft/s)

Inch-Pound to SI units

Multiply	By	To obtain
square mile (mi^2)	259.0	hectare (ha)
square mile (mi^2)	2.590	square kilometer (km^2)

Temperature in degrees Celsius (°C) may be converted to degrees Fahrenheit (°F) as follows: °F=(1.8×°C)+32.

Abbreviations, Acronyms, and Symbols

Abbreviations, Acronyms, and Symbols	Meaning
ADCP	Acoustic Doppler current profiler
AIC	Akaike's information criteria
ANOVA	Analysis of variance
CPUE	Catch per unit effort
CTD	Conductivity temperature depth profiler
dB	Decibel
DIN	Dissolved inorganic nitrogen
ESW	effective strip half width
FL	fork lengths
GIS	Geographic information systems
GLM	Generalized linear model
GLMM	Generalized linear mixed effects model
GPS	Global positioning system
IKMT	Isaacs-Kidd mid-water trawl
μM	Micro moles per liter
N:P	Nitrogen to phosphorous ratio
NASC	nautical area scattering coefficient
PAR	Photosynthetically active radiation

Kittlitz's and Marbled Murrelets in Kenai Fjords National Park, South-Central Alaska: At-Sea Distribution, Abundance, and Foraging Habitat, 2006–08

By M.L. Arimitsu, J.F. Piatt, M.D. Romano, E.N. Madison, and J.S. Conaway

Abstract

Kittlitz's murrelets (*Brachyramphus brevirostris*) and marbled murrelets (*B. marmoratus*) are small diving seabirds and are of management concern because of population declines in coastal Alaska. In 2006–08, we conducted a study in Kenai Fjords National Park, south-central Alaska, to estimate the recent population size of *Brachyramphus* murrelets, to evaluate productivity based on juvenile to adult ratios during the fledgling season, and to describe and compare their use of marine habitat. We also attempted a telemetry study to examine Kittlitz's murrelet nesting habitat requirements and at-sea movements. We estimated that the Kittlitz's murrelet population was 671 ± 144 birds, and the marbled murrelet population was 5,855 ± 1,163 birds. Kittlitz's murrelets were limited to the heads of three fjords with tidewater glaciers, whereas marbled murrelets were more widely distributed. Population estimates for both species were lower in 2007 than in 2006 and 2008, possibly because of anomalous oceanographic conditions that may have delayed breeding phenology. During late season surveys, we observed few hatch-year marbled murrelets and only a single hatch-year Kittlitz's murrelet over the course of the study. Using radio telemetry, we found a likely Kittlitz's murrelet breeding site on a mountainside bordering one of the fjords. We never observed radio-tagged Kittlitz's murrelets greater than 10 kilometer from their capture sites, suggesting that their foraging range during breeding is narrow. We observed differences in oceanography between fjords, reflecting differences in sill characteristics and orientation relative to oceanic influence. Acoustic biomass, a proxy for zooplankton and small schooling fish, generally decreased with distance from glaciers in Northwestern Lagoon, but was more variable in Aialik Bay where dense forage fish schools moved into glacial areas late in the summer. Pacific herring (*Clupea pallasii*), capelin (*Mallotus villosus*) and Pacific sand lance (*Ammodytes hexapterus*) were important forage species for murrelets in Kenai Fjords. Euphausiids also may have been an important forage resource for Kittlitz's murrelets in turbid glacial outflows in shallow waters during daytime. Marbled murrelets generally were more tolerant to a wider range of foraging habitat conditions although they tended to avoid the ice-covered silty waters close to glaciers. In contrast, Kittlitz's murrelets preferred areas where the influence of tidewater glaciers was the greatest and where their distribution was determined largely by prey availability. This work highlights an important link between interannual variability in murrelet counts at sea and mesoscale oceanographic conditions that influence marine productivity and prey distribution.

Introduction

Kittlitz's and marbled murrelets are non-colonial, diving seabirds of the Alcidae family. Like other alcids, *Brachyramphus* murrelets (hereafter referred to as murrelets) feed on small schooling fishes and invertebrates, have a long life span, and delay reproduction until they are several years old. The breeding range of the Kittlitz's murrelet is limited to Alaska and the Russian Far East, where they nest inland on talus slopes in glacial alpine or on unvegetated mountain slopes in deglaciated areas. Marbled murrelet breeding populations range from central California to southern Alaska and the Aleutian Islands, and they mostly nest inland in old-growth coniferous forests, usually on mossy tree limbs. In some areas, they nest on the ground. Both species are of management concern because of declining populations in core breeding areas Kissling and others, 2007; Piatt and others, 2007; Drew and Piatt, 2008; Kuletz and others, 2008; U.S. Fish and Wildlife Service, 2008).

Both species of murrelets co-occur in glacial fjords within coastal Alaska; however, marbled murrelets use a wider range of nearshore habitats. Distribution of Kittlitz's murrelets within glacial fjords of south-central and southeast Alaska is highly clumped with apparently persistent "hotspots" throughout the summer breeding season (Romano and others, 2004, 2006; Kissling and others, 2007). Kittlitz's murrelets were associated with strong tidal currents (Kissling and others, 2007) and preferred glacial-affected, nearshore, and highly turbid areas (Day and others, 2003). Marbled murrelets were more closely tied to shoreline habitats, and often associated with areas of upwelling near marine sills, mouths of bays, or eddies (Piatt and others, 2007).

Recent studies suggest breeding success of Kittlitz's murrelets in some areas of their breeding range was low (Day and Nigro, 2004; Kaler and others, 2009). Kaler and others (2009) estimated nesting success on an island in the western Aleutians at 0.06 ± 0.03 chicks/pair. This is much lower than estimates of 0.32 chicks/pair from direct observations of marbled murrelet nests throughout their range (Piatt and others, 2007) or of 0.48 chicks/pair (95% CI: 0.41–0.55) for marbled murrelets derived from telemetry studies in British Columbia (Bradley and others, 2004). The inaccessibility of murrelet nests adds to the difficulty of assessing reproductive success in most areas, and therefore, the ratio of juvenile to adult marbled murrelets observed at sea after fledging also has been used to provide an index of productivity (Strong, 1995; Kuletz and Piatt, 1999; Day and Nigro, 2004; Kuletz and others, 2008). In Kachemak Bay, juvenile marbled murrelet nursery areas were documented during late-season surveys (Kuletz and Piatt, 1999; Kuletz and others, 2008), although the occurrence and timing of juvenile Kittlitz's murrelets at sea is still poorly known.

Because of population declines in Kittlitz's murrelet's core areas of distribution, the U.S. Fish and Wildlife Service (USFWS) designated the seabird as a candidate for listing under the Endangered Species Act (69 FR 24875-24904). Marbled murrelets are currently (as of 2010) listed as threatened from British Columbia to California, but not in Alaska (McShane and others, 2004; Piatt and others, 2007). In Kenai Fjords National Park, surveys conducted between 1976 and 2002 suggested that the population of Kittlitz's Murrelets declined by as much as 83 percent during that time (Van Pelt and Piatt, 2003). In contrast, *Brachyramphus* murrelet populations (including a large proportion of unidentified murrelets) in adjacent Prince William Sound have declined by 60 percent in recent decades (Piatt and others, 2007). Similarly, in Kachemak Bay, *Brachyramphus* murrelets declined by 32 percent between 1993 and 2005 (Kuletz and others, 2008). Leading hypotheses to explain all or part of the decline include naturally occurring changes in food abundance, glacial recession, oil spill mortality, vessel disturbance in foraging areas, and gillnet mortality.

The study area covered the coastal area of Kenai Fjords, Alaska, extending from Callisto Head in the east to Gore Point in the west (fig. 1). The outer portion of each fjord is exposed to Gulf of Alaska currents, whereas the inner portions are influenced by runoff from glaciers extending from the Harding Icefield. For the marine habitat part of this study, two fjords are of interest because of resident summer populations of Kittlitz's murrelets—Aialik Bay and Northwestern Lagoon. Each fjord contains a sill, which is a neoglacial terminal moraine shoal at the position of the glacier terminus during the Little Ice Age maximum (Wiles and others, 1995). Glacial retreat in Aialik Bay occurred around the late 1600s, and ice retreat in Northwestern Lagoon began around the late 1800s (Wiles and others, 1995).

The goal of this study was to examine variability in the at-sea distribution, abundance, and habitat use of Kittlitz's and marbled murrelets during the breeding season (June–August) in the nearshore waters adjacent to Kenai Fjords National Park, Alaska. The objectives of the study were (1) to determine the population status of *Brachyramphus* murrelets in Kenai Fjords, (2) to attempt to assess productivity based on at-sea surveys, and (3) to contrast the use of different marine habitats by the two murrelet species.

This report summarizes a 3-year study on the distribution and abundance of Kittlitz's murrelets and marbled murrelets in waters adjacent to Kenai Fjords National Park, Alaska. Here, we summarize results from systematic, at-sea surveys in the Kenai Fjords during the summers of 2006–08. In addition, we present results from a pilot radio telemetry effort in 2006, and foraging habitat studies in 2007–08. Finally, we discuss factors related to survey design, and interannual and within season variability in murrelet counts.

Methods

During each year of the study, we conducted surveys in the early, middle, and late periods of the breeding season for murrelets (table 1). Data were collected using a combination of boat-based marine bird surveys, oceanographic surveys, nearshore (less than 30 m from shore) and offshore (greater than 200 m from shore) fish sampling using beach seines and Isaacs-Kidd mid-water trawls (IKMT), hydroacoustic surveys for fish and zooplankton biomass, and measurements of tidal current velocity using an acoustic Doppler current profiler (ADCP) near glacial features. In 2006, we attempted to characterize Kittlitz's murrelet foraging habitat by using radio telemetry to locate birds at sea. However, only small numbers of Kittlitz's murrelets were found and captured so this effort was not cost effective. The telemetry component of this study was eliminated for 2007 and 2008. In lieu of a telemetry effort, we focused our effort on characterizing foraging habitat of murrelets in Aialik Bay and Northwestern Lagoon. We intended to also include marine bird surveys in the East Arm of Nuka Bay during each sampling period; however, weather and logistical constraints precluded surveys in the area during the early season in 2008, and late season in 2006 and 2008. Likewise, poor weather and other logistical constraints prevented us from conducting dedicated productivity surveys in 2008.

At-Sea Surveys

To document the distribution and abundance of *Brachyramphus* murrelets in Kenai Fjords, the coastal and offshore areas of Kenai Fjords were sampled during the 2006–08 breeding seasons (fig. 2). Coastwide surveys were conducted in the middle (late June to mid-July) of the expected breeding season in order to estimate the recent (2006-08) population size of Kittlitz's and marbled murrelets. We did attempt to schedule surveys as early as possible during this time period (that is, starting in late June) but scheduling a vessel for the work at that time was not always possible. Aialik Bay, Northwestern Lagoon, and when possible, the East Arm of Nuka Bay, also were surveyed early in the season (late May-early June) and later in the season (early to mid-August) to characterize the abundance and distribution of both murrelet species during the breeding season (table 1).

In 2006, a systematic sampling design with a combination of coastal and offshore transects was established. The coastal transects were created by dividing the entire coastline of Kenai Fjords National Park and the adjacent islands (from Callisto Head to Gore Point) into 4-km segments using a geographic information system (GIS). After selecting a random starting point, one out of every three of the 4-km segments was systematically selected to be surveyed. To create the offshore transects for the survey, parallel lines running from east to west and spaced every 0.93 km (30 seconds of latitude) were drawn for each major bay along the Kenai Fjords coast. Because previous surveys indicated that Kittlitz's murrelet distribution is restricted to the upper sections of Aialik Bay and in Northwestern Lagoon, coverage of these areas was increased. Offshore transects in Upper Aialik Bay and Northwestern Lagoon were spaced every 1.9 km (1 minute of latitude).

All surveys were conducted following strip survey protocols established by the U.S. Fish and Wildlife Service for surveying marine birds (Gould and Forsell, 1989), with modification for working in coastal nearshore waters from small boats (Agler and others, 1998) and continuously counting flying birds. All surveys in 2006 were conducted from a 4.8 m Naiad® rigid-hulled inflatable skiff. In 2007, surveys within more exposed waters were conducted from the 15.6 m M/V *Alaskan Gyre*. In 2008, the subset of transects (fig. 2), repeated in Aialik Bay and Northwestern Lagoon during early, middle, and late-season sampling periods, was surveyed from the M/V *Alaskan Gyre* to accommodate concurrent shipboard hydroacoustic and thermosalinograph sampling (see section "Marine Habitat"). For all survey periods and vessel types in 2006 and 2007, two observers identified birds and mammals within 100 m of either side or 200 m forward of the vessel, resulting in a 200 m wide survey strip. In 2008, strip-width for transects conducted from the M/V *Alaskan Gyre* (only) were increased to 300 m effective width (150 m on either side of the vessel) because of improved sighting conditions at increased observer altitude (Becker and others, 1999). Ground speed when conducting surveys generally was held between 9 and 22 km/h. Speed during bird surveys conducted concurrently with hydroacoustics (see section, "Hydroacoustics") generally was held between 9 and 11 km/h.

All birds and mammals were identified to species whenever possible. Identification of murrelets within the genus *Brachyramphus* can be particularly difficult given the similarity in size, shape, and plumage. Survey crews slowed the vessel when necessary to confirm identification of murrelets. A behavior code was assigned to all birds and mammals sighted on transect as either on the water (swimming on surface), fish-holding (holding fish in bill), or flying. Bird and mammal sightings were recorded by entering them directly into a real-time computer data-entry system (dLOG-CE v.1.5.0; Glenn Ford Consulting, Portland, OR) that logs sightings continuously along with their GPS coordinates. A waterproof, shock-proof, GPS-enabled hand-held computer (TDS Recon®) was used for data entry. Two observers actively scanned ahead of and alongside the survey vessel, and species identifications were confirmed using 8–10 power binoculars. Weather conditions and sea state were constantly monitored and surveys were not conducted if wave height exceeded 0.5 m in height.

For *Brachyramphus* murrelets only, the perpendicular distance from the transect line to each bird or group of birds also was estimated in order to compare densities observed using standard strip and line transect analysis methodology. Although special attention was paid to the centerline to ensure all birds were counted, we attempted to estimate distance to all murrelets sighted to a maximum distance of 100 m in 2006 and 2007, and a maximum of 300 m in 2008. Observer training was conducted prior to each survey using a combination of range finders on fixed objects, and bird-sized buoys strung at known distances on a line towed behind the vessel. Distance calibration with range finders was reinforced daily throughout each survey. In 2007, grouped distance observations (0–20 m, 21–40 m, 41–60 m, 61–80 m, 81–100 m) were recorded, whereas in 2006 and 2008, exact distance observations were recorded.

Productivity Surveys

Productivity of murrelets was estimated using juvenile to adult ratios from late summer counts following Kuletz and Piatt (1999). Productivity surveys in 2006 included a survey of the subset of transects in upper Aialik Bay and Northwestern Lagoon on August 12–14 (table 1, fig. 2), where most fledglings were sighted nearshore. In 2007, the entire shoreline within Aialik Bay and Northwestern Lagoon was surveyed on multiple days (fig. 3). Weather and logistical constraints hampered dedicated fledgling survey efforts in 2008; however, late season surveys corresponded with the timing of murrelet fledging period in nearby Prince William Sound and Kachemak Bay (Kuletz and Piatt, 1999; Kuletz and others, 2008). During productivity surveys, all murrelets sighted within 100 m of either side of a 4.8 m skiff were identified, enumerated, and assigned a plumage and life stage. Perpendicular distances to birds were not recorded. Boat speed was usually held between 9 and 22 km/h, but observers stopped the boat when necessary to improve accuracy in species and life stage identification. To improve comparisons among years, the productivity datasets were refined to include only observations from coastal transects that were surveyed in all years. A productivity index (fledglings/adults) was calculated by dividing the number of juveniles observed by the number of adults observed.

Telemetry

In May 2006, we attempted to capture 20 birds of each species using the night-lighting technique (Whitworth and others, 1997) for a radio-telemetry study. We were only able to capture eight Kittlitz's murrelets and no marbled murrelets. All birds captured were weighed, and we measured lengths of tarsus, flattened wing chord, culmen, and total length of head and bill combined. Each bird also was inspected for a brood patch and the stage if development was noted.

Radio-transmitters (model A4360; Advanced Telemetry Systems Inc.®, Isanti, MN) were attached to all captured Kittlitz's murrelets dorsally with commercial-grade adhesive (Slo-Zap® cyanoacrylate; Pacer Technology, Rancho Cucamonga, CA) and a subcutaneous anchor, following Newman and others (1999). Previous radio-telemetry studies of marbled murrelets in British Columbia have reported transmitter retention times of 3 to 18 months using this attachment method (Nadine Parker, Simon Frasier University, oral commun., 2006; Russell Bradley, Simon Frasier University, oral commun., 2006). The transmitters were mounted along the dorsal mid-line of each bird and centered between the scapulae. The model A4360 transmitters weigh approximately 3.2 g, which equals less than 2 percent of the mean body mass of Kittlitz's murrelet adults (238 ± 4 g, n = 20) captured during a previous study in Glacier Bay National Park (Romano and others, 2007b). To decrease the amount of wing-loading stress, transmitter mass should not exceed 2–3 percent of body mass for flying birds (Kenwood, 2001).

Surveys were done from small boats and fixed-wing aircraft to relocate radio-tagged birds. The primary vessel for the boat surveys was a 4.8 m Naiad® rigid-hulled inflatable. Boat-based surveys were limited to Aialik Bay, Harris Bay, and Northwestern Lagoon and were done opportunistically as weather and time allowed. During boat-based surveys a radio receiver (model R2000; Advanced Telemetry Systems Inc., Isanti, MN) was connected to a hand-held three-element Yagi® antennae. One observer monitored the receiver while a second observer scanned the water with binoculars looking for birds.

Aerial telemetry surveys were done from a Cessna® 305A equipped with two wing strut-mounted H antennas with a radio receiver connected to the antennas through a switch box (Kenwood, 2001). This arrangement facilitates more efficient tracking of signals because the observer can determine which side of the aircraft a signal is coming from by listening through each antenna independently and comparing the strength of the signals. Eight telemetry flights were flown from May 26 through July 1, 2006. Flights departed from Seward or Homer, Alaska, and covered the coastal area between Seward and Nuka Bay during each flight. The entire length of each bay along the coast was flown at an average altitude of between 600 and 900 m. The flights also covered the ice-free upland area in each bay between the water and the Harding Icefield (fig. 4). The flights originating in Homer covered a broad region including Kachemak Bay, the southwest corner of the Kenai Peninsula, and the upland area between Kachemak Bay and Nuka Bay.

Marine Habitat

Marine habitat characteristics within Aialik Bay and Northwestern Lagoon were examined during the 2007 and 2008 field seasons. Sampling covered approximately 25 km from the face of the glaciers to the outer fjord stations in each fjord. In July 2007, a pilot study was done to measure marine habitat characteristics using a stratified random sampling approach, and in 2008, a monthly systematic sampling approach was used to increase effort along established oceanography stations and bird survey transects. Sampling included oceanographic measurements, ichthyoplankton and zooplankton collections, water samples, and hydroacoustics.

Oceanography

Oceanographic gradients in the marine environment were measured by conducting oceanography surveys at sample sites established by Gay and Armato (1998) in Aialik Bay and Northwestern Lagoon (fig. 5). In 2007, oceanographic surveys were done in conjunction with early and late-season bird surveys. In 2008, oceanographic surveys also coincided with the timing of hydroacoustic surveys (described below). At each station, we deployed a conductivity-temperature-depth profiler (CTD, SeaBird Electronics® SBE-19) equipped with a fluorometer (WetLabs® WetStar). In June and July 2008, additional sensors were used, including a dissolved oxygen sensor (SeaBird Electronics® SBE-43), photosynthetically active radiation (PAR) sensor (Biospherical® Quantum Scalar 2300L), and a beam transmissometer (WetLabs® C-STAR). In August 2008, all external sensors failed and only CTD data were available.

Environmental and biological parameters were sampled in 2008 at a subset of oceanographic stations including two inner-fjord and two outer fjord stations, hereinafter referred to as glacial and distal stations, respectively (fig. 5). A water sampler (Seabird Electronics® SBE 55) was deployed in conjunction with the CTD and water samples were collected at discrete depths of 2 and 10 m. Nutrient samples from 2 and 10 m depths were frozen in the field and analyzed for ammonium (NH_4^+), phosphate (PO_4^{3-}), silicic acid ($Si(OH)_4$), nitrate (NO_3^-), and nitrite (NO_2^-) concentrations at the Marine Chemistry Lab of the University of Washington.

Tidal Current Velocity

Tidal current velocities were mapped in Aialik and Northwestern Lagoons on August 14–17, 2007, using a 600 kHz acoustic Doppler current profiler interfaced with a differentially corrected GPS. Typically, lower frequency units are used in marine applications, but the higher frequency unit was better suited for shallow and high velocity conditions found at the submerged moraines. Measurements of tidal discharge were made at the submerged glacial moraine that separates Northwestern Lagoon and Harris Bay, and at the submerged glacial moraine that extends from Pedersen Lagoon to Coleman Bay in Aialik Bay. The acoustic Doppler current profiler was deployed using a small trimaran that was towed by an inflatable boat. Data were collected during peak ebb and flood tides and at slack tide. The path of data collection was normal to the primary direction of tidal flow. This cross-section pattern provided a quantification of tidal discharge fluxing in and out of the fjords during tidal shifts. Concurrent conductivity, temperature, depth, and salinity measurements were made with each cross section.

Zooplankton

Mid-water trawls were done to assess community structure of prey relative to glacial features in Aialik Bay and Northwestern Lagoon. In 2007, a large IKMT was deployed at 21 randomly selected stations stratified by distance to glacial features in Aialik Bay and Northwestern Lagoon during a cruise from June 29 to July 3 (fig. 6). The large IKMT was 6 m long with a 3.05 m depressor bar, 7.68 m^2 mouth opening, and 3 mm knotless nylon mesh. The collection cup at the cod end had 1 mm mesh screen. Each station was sampled for 30 minutes, for an average transect length (± SD) of 2.9 ± 0.38 km. This net was effective at catching ichthyoplankton and macrozooplankton, but the large depressor bar made the net more difficult to deploy and so a smaller net was used in 2008.

In 2008, a smaller IKMT was deployed at the same subset of oceanography stations described above (fig. 5). The small IKMT was outfitted with 1.8 m depressor bar, 3 mm stretched knotless mesh near the mouth, and a 333-μm mesh ring net, which comprised approximately two-thirds of the body including the cod end. The net was deployed in an oblique manner and outfitted with a depth sensor (VEMCO® minilog T data logger, or Star Oddi® DST CTD) to assess the maximum trawl depth. A flowmeter (General Oceanics®) was attached to the mouth of the net to estimate distance through the water. Maximum depth towed was 35 m, average (± SD) distance towed was 1.2 ± 0.1 km, and speed during the tow was held at approximately 5.5 km/h. One outer station in Harris Bay could not be sampled with the IKMT during the early-season cruise because of inclement weather.

For both types of IKMT hauls, total catch volume was estimated to the nearest 10 mL after water was drained through sieves. Gelatinous zooplankton, including ctenophores and cnidarians, were separated and their volume was estimated as above. Individual ctenophores and cnidarians were not identified to species or enumerated as a result of damage to individuals during capture. All fish collected in IKMT hauls were identified to species and fork lengths (FL) were measured to the nearest 1.0 mm. Fish that could not be identified in the field were preserved in 10 percent formaldehyde in seawater solution and returned to the laboratory for later identification.

Small zooplankton species were sampled with a 211 μm, 0.6 m ring net on a 50 m (or to within 5 m from the bottom) vertical haul at the end of each IKMT haul in 2007 and 2008. Volume filtered was measured with a flowmeter (General Oceanics®).

IKMT and ringnet zooplankton sample contents were preserved in a 3–5 percent buffered formaldehyde and seawater solution. Samples were identified to species (or lowest possible taxon) and developmental stage, enumerated, and damp dry weights measured to the nearest 0.01 mg (or for organisms weighing more than 100 mg, to the nearest milligram) under contract with the University of Alaska Fairbanks. After rare organisms were removed and counted, large samples were subsampled with a Folsom® plankton splitter.

Hydroacoustics

In June, July, and August 2008, biomass of fish, zooplankton, and other nekton taxa were estimated during hydroacoustic surveys that were done concurrently with seabird surveys at a subset of transects in Aialik Bay and Northwestern Fjord (fig. 2). A single beam, 120 kHz transducer (Biosonics DT-X®) deployed from a hydrodynamic fin was towed along side of the boat at an approximate depth of 2 m below the surface. The vessel generally traveled at speeds between 9 and 11 km/h; however, ice obstructions near the head of the fjords forced us to slow the vessel to 5 km/h at times. The instrument had a beam angle of 6.5° and collected data at 2 pings/s and with a pulse length of 0.5 ms. Field calibration was conducted according to Foote and others (1987) on June 2 and July 11, 2008, using a 33 mm standard calibration sphere of known target strength. During hydroacoustic/bird transects, a thermosalinograph (Seabird Electronics® SBE 45 MicroTSG) was deployed to identify surface temperature and salinity conditions.

Nearshore Fish

Nearshore fish were sampled with a beach seine at beaches suitable for seining and near foraging birds (fig. 5). The beach seine was 37 m long, with mesh size between 28 mm at the wings and 5 mm at the center. The seine was set parallel to shore from a skiff and retrieved from the beach by two or three people. The catch was put into a holding bucket, identified, counted, and as many as 25 haphazardly selected individuals from each species were measured (fork length in millimeters). At each site, we recorded location coordinates, sediment type, incline of beach (high, moderate, low), and percent cover of kelp swept with the net.

Data Analysis

Mid-season transects were stratified in relation to their position relative to the sills in Aialik Bay, Northwestern Lagoon, and the East Arm of Nuka Bay (fig. 7). The "Fjords" strata consisted of coastal (less than 200 m from shore) and offshore (greater than 200 m from shore) transects north of the prominent marine sills within Aialik Bay, Northwestern Lagoon, and the East Arm of Nuka Bay (fig. 1). The "Bays" strata consisted of coastal and offshore transects outside of the Fjords strata (fig. 7). These strata were selected *a priori* because previous work in Kenai Fjords had shown that murrelet density and distribution differed with distance to shoreline and relation to marine sills (Van Pelt and Piatt, 2003). ArcGIS v. 9.2 (ESRI®, Redlands, CA, USA) software was used to create the strata and estimate area within each stratum.

A population estimate was generated for Kittlitz's, marbled, and all *Brachyramphus* murrelets from the mid-season survey data stratified by area for each year using Program Distance® v. 6.0 (Thomas and others, 2009). For analyses of line transect and strip transect data, observations were truncated at 100 m to allow comparisons with survey periods and with previous surveys. Densities of birds on the water were estimated using line transect methodology and densities of birds in the air were estimated using strip transect methodology. Flying birds were not included in line transect estimates because of the difficulty of estimating perpendicular distance to flying birds, and because detection of flying birds would differ from that of stationary birds. A final population estimate was calculated as the sum of the stratified line transect estimate for birds on the water and stratified strip transect estimate for birds in the air.

For line transect estimates of birds on the water, detections were modeled as clusters, or observations of single or groups of birds sitting on the water. Detection functions for line transects are not reliable with fewer than 60–80 detections (Buckland and others, 2001), and in some or all strata-year combinations, there were not enough detections by species for a robust sighting probability model. Therefore, a global detection function for all *Brachyramphus* murrelets was applied to each species' distance data for each stratum-year combination. If the sighting probability of murrelets in coastal strata was less than one at 100 m from the transect line, we applied the detection function for offshore transects (Kissling and others, 2007). Candidate models included uniform and half-normal keys with cosine, polynomial, or hermite adjustment terms. The most parsimonious sighting probability models were selected on the basis of Akaike Information Criterion (AIC) values. Strip transect estimates of flying birds were modeled using a uniform key and cosine adjustment. For all models, variance was estimated empirically, cluster size was determined by the mean, and non-parametric bootstrap was applied by resampling samples within strata 999 times (Efron and Tibshirani, 1986). Pooled densities were calculated as the mean of stratum density weighted by stratum area, and population size was calculated as the sum of stratum density multiplied by stratum area. Log-based confidence intervals were computed according to Buckland and others (2001).

Early, middle, and late season densities of murrelets were calculated using a ratio estimator (Agler and others, 1998; Kuletz and others, 2008) for a subset of transects repeated in Aialik Bay and Northwestern Lagoon for each year (fig. 2). For each survey, distance data were used to estimate a detection function for all *Brachyramphus* murrelets on offshore transects, and the resulting effective strip half width (ESW) was used to correct stratified density estimates when the sighting probability was less than 1 across the 200 m strip width. Raw counts of birds were prorated to proportionately allocate unidentified birds into density estimates of each murrelet species, using the ratio between Kittlitz's and Marbled murrelets positively identified on a transect-by-transect basis. After summing the count of birds by transect, and setting a single interval distance at the ESW for offshore transects, stratified density estimates were computed using a uniform key and cosine adjustment in Program Distance®. Within-season density was calculated for raw and prorated counts of Kittlitz's and Marbled Murrelets. A productivity index was calculated for Kittlitz's and Marbled murrelets following Kuletz and Piatt (1999), including only coastal transects repeated in each year. A t-test was used to compare measurements of captured birds from Kenai Fjords in 2006 to captured birds from Glacier Bay National Park in 2004 (Romano and others, 2007a).

Raw CTD data were processed through SBE Data Processing modules v. 7.18 (Sea-Bird Electronics, Bellevue, WA, USA). Photic depth was calculated as the depth at which PAR values dropped to 1 percent of surface values. Water column profile data were contoured in MATLAB® v. 7.5 (MathWorks, Natick, MA, USA) relative to depth and station distance along a line drawn between the head of the fjord and the outer-most station.

Spatial and temporal differences in abiotic and biotic datasets were tested with two-way or three-way fixed effects ANOVA using JMP® v. 7.0.2 (SAS Institute, Cary, NC, USA), including within fjord (glacial versus distal), between fjord (Northwestern versus Aialik), and month factors. Response variables were tested for normality using Shapiro-Wilks, and homogeneity of variance was assessed through residual plots and Levene's tests at $\alpha < 0.05$. For multi-factorial tests, when interaction terms were not significant, additive models were applied. Data were transformed to induce normality, or a Spearman rank correlation was used when assumptions of normality and homoscedasticity were not satisfied.

Multivariate statistical analyses of trawl catch community structure were conducted in PRIMER® v. 6 (PRIMER-E Ltd & PERMANOVA 1.0.1, Lutten, Ivybridge, UK). Prior to analysis of trawl catch community structure, we reduced the dataset to include species that are important in murrelet diets, including euphausiids, copepods (by species), shrimp, amphipods, capelin, and gadids. Gelatinous zooplankton also were included because they likely influenced community structure and associations with Kittlitz's murrelets have been observed in Glacier Bay (J. Piatt, US Geological Survey, unpublished data, 2004). The Bray-Curtis similarity measure was computed on abundance data that were first log (x+1) transformed and standardized. We tested for homogeneity of multivariate dispersions in species composition between levels of factors. Factors included glacial influence (glacial versus distal stations), month, and location (Aialik versus Northwestern). Homogeneity of multivariate dispersions was met for glacial influence (PERMDISP: $F_{[1,21]} = 3.97$, $p = 0.07$) and location (PERMDISP: $F_{[1,21]} = 0.63$, $p = 0.47$) factors, but it was rejected for the month factor (PERMDISP: $F_{[1,21]} = 4.00$, $p = 0.05$). Pairwise tests indicated July and August samples were not significantly different from one another ($p = 0.27$). A 3-way fixed effects permutation-based MANOVA was used to test for differences in zooplankton species composition. When interaction terms were not significant at $\alpha = 0.05$, additive models were used. Contributions of individual species to community structure were examined using the SIMPER routine.

Hydroacoustic data were integrated with Echoview® v. 2.10 software (SonarData Pty. Ltd., Hobart, Tasmania, AUS). Noise was reduced by setting a minimum threshold for integration at -80 dB. Sound speed and absorption coefficients were determined from CTD casts. Surface noise and the bottom signal, determined by visually examining the echograms, were excluded from the analysis. Additionally, the data for the upper 1 m were removed to eliminate the effects of collecting data in the near field of the transducer, which resulted in the effective minimum depth of acoustic measurements at 3 m below the surface. The integration output for acoustic backscatter was expressed as nautical area scattering coefficient (NASC), and was used as a proxy for biomass. NASC was summed over the upper 40 m ($NASC_{40}$) of the water column to estimate biomass available within the diving depth of Kittlitz's murrelets (maximum approximately 35–40 m, Day and others, 1999). $NASC_{40}$ over the length of each transect was summed and divided by the transect length (sum of $NASC_{40}$ / km) to standardize by effort. Distance from the midpoint of each acoustic transect to the nearest tidewater glacier was estimated in GIS. A 2-way ANOVA was applied to acoustic data summed by transect to test for differences between fjords and months. Least squares linear regression was used to examine the relationship between the log-transformed sum of $NASC_{40}$ / km and the transect distance to nearest tidewater glacier by month and fjord.

To assess changes in schooling fish distribution over the course of the 2008 breeding season, dense fish aggregations were separated from more dispersed prey and weaker scattering targets as in Mehlum and others (1996). Dense forage fish aggregations encountered on hydroacoustic surveys were integrated by month by visually examining the echograms, identifying regions containing dense aggregations of fish, and integrating aggregations separately from weaker scattering organisms, such as zooplankton and dispersed fish. Dense schools of fish typically are distinct in their shape and target strength characteristics compared to weaker scattering organisms (Simmonds and MacLennan, 2005).

To relate Kittlitz's and marbled murrelet distribution in Aialik Bay and Northwestern Lagoon to environmental variables, we used a combination of generalized linear models (GLM) and generalized linear mixed effects models (GLMM) using survey data, bathymetry, and concurrent hydroacoustic and thermosalinograph data from July 2008. Raw point data from marine bird and acoustic transects in Aialik Bay and Northwestern Lagoon (fig. 2) were divided into 200, 400, 800, and 1,600 m segments, aggregated by segment, and analyzed using R statistical software v. 2.7.2 (R development Core Team, 2008). For each distance class, the response variable was presence/absence of murrelets (by species) within each segment, and independent variables were calculated as the mean acoustic biomass, sea surface salinity, and bottom depth within each segment. Distance from the midpoint of each transect segment to the nearest tidewater glacier also was included as an explanatory variable. Ice presence/absence, fjord (Aialik Bay or Northwestern Lagoon), and transect type (coastal or offshore) were coded as a categorical variables. Prior to analysis, we log $(x + 0.0001)$-transformed mean acoustic biomass and then normalized continuous variables. Sea surface temperature was not included as an independent variable because it was highly correlated with glacier distance. The presence or absence of murrelets was coded as a binary response (0/1) and the probability of observing murrelets along a given segment was modeled as a function of the predictor variables using a GLM with a binomial error distribution and a logit link. The best GLM models were selected on the basis of AIC values. Kittlitz's murrelets were never present where ice was absent; modeling of habitat preferences was therefore restricted to those observations where ice was present. To account for spatial autocorrelation between segments on a single transect, we followed the exploration of candidate GLM models with GLMM models that incorporated spatial autocorrelation within transects and allowed for random differences in the mean response (probability of occurrence) among transects (Dormann and others, 2007). The correlation structure was modeled as an exponential spatial correlation using the following equation:

$$f(d_{ij}) = \exp\left(\frac{-d_{ij}}{p}\right) \qquad (1)$$

where
dij is equal to the distance between two observations, and
p is the range coefficient.
The performance of the final models in predicting presence/absence of murrelets was evaluated based on the proportion of fitted probabilities that resulted in correct classification of the response (presence/absence), whereby a predicted probability of greater than or equal to 0.5 was considered to indicate presence. Although we examined models at multiple scales, only the most parsimonious model with the highest correct prediction rate for each species is presented.

Results

Population, Distribution, and Abundance

During the 2006–08 murrelet breeding seasons, a total of 506 transects and a sampling area of 416 km^2 were surveyed (table 1). To estimate the population of murrelets in Kenai Fjords, we surveyed between 11.9 and 12.8 percent of the total area with 100, 90, and 99 transects in 2006, 2007, and 2008, respectively (table 2).

We counted 7,879 murrelets over the course of this study, of which Kittlitz's murrelets comprised 8.9 percent, marbled murrelets 87.1 percent and unidentified *Brachyramphus* murrelets 3.9 percent of all observations. Data were collected on all marine birds and mammals sighted during the surveys and total counts of those observations are presented in appendixes 1–3.

The overall mean group size (± SE) for Kittlitz's murrelets was 1.59 ± 0.07 birds/group and was slightly higher for marbled murrelets at 1.99 ± 0.03 birds/group. Group size ranged from 1 to 11 birds/group for Kittlitz's murrelets and 1 to 50 birds/ group for marbled murrelets.

Kittlitz's Murrelets

We estimated that the population (and 95% CI) of Kittlitz's murrelets in Kenai Fjords National Park was 925 (393–2,179) birds in 2006, 423 (252–709) birds in 2007, and 664 (294–1,499) birds in 2008 (table 3). Between 0 and 19.8 percent of birds observed flying during surveys were identified as Kittlitz's murrelets (table 4).

Marbled Murrelets

The estimated population of marbled murrelets was 6,418 (4,730–8,709) birds in 2006, 3,619 (2,371–5,524) birds in 2007, and 7,529 (5,546–10,222) birds in 2008 (table 3). Marbled murrelets comprised between 0.6 and 4.7 percent of all flying murrelets (table 4).

Brachyramphus Murrelets

Total population estimates for all *Brachyramphus* murrelets in Kenai Fjords were 7,586 (5,344–10,768) in 2006; 4,424 (3,099–6,315) in 2007; and 9,677 (7,449–12,571) in 2008 (table 3). Unidentified *Brachyramphus* murrelets comprised between 10.8 and 82.4 percent of flying murrelet observations (table 4).

Density

Density estimates for all Kittlitz's murrelets sighted within 100 m of either side of the vessel on the subset of transects repeated in Aialik Bay and Northwestern Lagoon during all years were on average (± SE) 2.74 (± 0.27) birds/km^2 in the early season, 2.67 (± 0.67) birds/km^2 for mid-season, and 1.10 (± 0.35) birds/km^2 for late season surveys (table 5). In 2006 and 2008, Kittlitz's murrelet density increased from early to mid-season, followed by a decrease late in the season. In 2007, density decreased between early and mid-season, and late season density remained relatively stable through late-season surveys. Additionally, in 2007, late season density was higher although the coefficient of variation was lower than in 2006 and 2008 (table 5). During mid-season coastwide surveys, the average density for Kittlitz's murrelets was highest in the fjord offshore stratum (table 6, fig. 8), with average density (± SE) of 5.97 (± 1.58) birds/km^2 across years, and it was lowest in the bays offshore stratum with an average (± SE) density of 0.02 (± 0.02) birds/km^2 across years. When raw counts of Kittlitz's murrelets were prorated for unidentified birds, average densities were 2.91 (0.34) birds/km^2 in the early season, 2.85 (0.66) birds/km^2 in the mid-season, and 1.18 (0.43) birds/km^2 in the late season (table 5). Prorated estimates increased Kittlitz's Murrelet within-season density estimates by an average of 5.6 (2.9) percent. Lowest variability in Kittlitz's Murrelet density occurred in the early season surveys (table 5).

Density estimates for all marbled murrelets on transects repeated throughout the 2006–08 summers were on average (± SE) 13.75 (± 2.75) birds/km^2 in the early season, 15.72 (± 1.68) birds/km^2 in the mid-season, and 33.88 (± 7.18) birds/km^2 in the late season (table 5). Coefficients of variation ranged from 19.7 to 32.8% in the early season, 24.8 to 38.1 percent in the mid-season, and 21.3 to 21.6 percent in the late season. Similar to Kittlitz's murrelets density patterns, marbled murrelets had lowest densities in the early season compared to middle and late season estimates in 2006 and 2008, whereas monthly densities were lowest during the mid-season survey in 2007. The highest density of marbled murrelets occurred during the late season survey in 2007, with an average (± SE) of 46.77 (± 9.98) birds/km^2. During mid-season coastwide surveys, average density of marbled murrelets was highest in the fjord coastal stratum (table 6, fig. 9). When raw counts were prorated for unidentified birds, average density of Marbled Murrelets was 14.33 (3.09) birds/km^2 in the early season, 16.46 (2.22) birds/km^2 in the mid-season, and 35.31 (7.97) birds/km^2 in the late season (table 5). Prorating counts increased Marbled Murrelet within-season density estimates by an average of 3.6 (1.9) percent. Lowest variability in Marbled Murrelet density occurred during the mid-season surveys (table 5). During mid-season coastwide surveys, the average (± SE) marbled murrelets density for all years was highest in the fjord coastal stratum (table 6) with 25.32 (± 4.00) birds/km^2, and lowest in the bays offshore stratum with 7.15 (± 1.85) birds/km^2.

Productivity

A total of 421 adults and 13 marbled murrelet fledglings were observed on transects in Northwestern Lagoon and Aialik Bay on August 12–14, 2006. The majority of marbled murrelet fledglings (85 percent) were sighted on coastal transects (fig. 10). Seven adult and no Kittlitz's murrelet fledglings were observed on transect.

In 2007, we covered 172.6 linear km for a survey area of 34.5 km^2 during the first set of transects on August 9–11, and 84.0 linear km for a survey area of 16.8 km^2 during the second set of transects on August 14–17. A total of 51 adult Kittlitz's murrelets were observed during fledgling surveys in 2007. Twenty-nine adults in alternate plumage and one adult in basic plumage were sighted during the first juvenile survey, and 21 adults in alternate plumage were sighted during the second juvenile survey. One adult was observed holding a juvenile Pacific herring in Northwestern Lagoon on August 16, 2007. No hatch-year or possible hatch-year Kittlitz's murrelets were observed in 2007. The majority of Kittlitz's murrelets were sighted in the glaciated area near the head of Northwestern Lagoon.

During fledgling surveys in 2007, we observed 1,866 adult, 5 hatch-year, and 1 possible hatch-year marbled murrelets. Three adults were in basic plumage, one adult was in intermediate plumage, and the remaining adults were in alternate plumage. Ten adults were carrying fish—one carrying a capelin, eight each carrying a juvenile Pacific herring, and one carrying a Pacific sand lance.

In 2008, 15 adults, and a single juvenile Kittlitz's murrelet were observed on late season surveys in Aialik Bay and Northwestern Lagoon. The juvenile Kittlitz's murrelet was the only fledgling observed during the course of the study, and its identification was confirmed with a photograph. There were 556 adult marbled murrelets, one fledgling, and two possible fledglings sighted on transect. All adult Kittlitz's murrelets, and all but one adult marbled murrelet were in alternate plumage. We observed 1 Kittlitz's murrelet and 16 marbled murrelets carrying fish, but no fish were identified to species.

A productivity index (juvenile: adult ratio for surveys data effort was repeated during all 3 years) for Kittlitz's murrelets was 0 in 2006 and 2007, and 0.1 fledglings/adult in 2008. A productivity index for marbled murrelets for the same coastal area was 0.03 fledglings/adult in 2006, 0.01 fledglings/adult in 2007, and 0.002 (0.006 if possible hatch year birds are included) fledglings/adult in 2008.

Observations of Radio-Marked Kittlitz's Murrelets

Eight Kittlitz's murrelets were captured during the night on the water between May 7 and 13, 2006. Two of the birds were caught as a pair, in a single scoop of the dipnet. Of the single birds captured, most were sighted on the water with a partner but only one of the pair was pursued. The weather, sea conditions, and extent of ice greatly limited capture possibilities and success. The capture success rate was less than 50 percent for birds positively identified on the water. Rain and sea conditions limited the visibility of the observers and sea conditions also limited the maneuverability of the capture vessel.

The body measurements of the 8 birds captured in Kenai Fjords were compared to a sample of 20 Kittlitz's murrelets that were captured in Glacier Bay National Park during May 2004. The birds captured in Kenai Fjords had significantly lower body mass than birds captured in Glacier Bay ($p < 0.05$; table 7). In contrast, there was no difference between the two groups in length of tarsus ($p = 0.09$), wing ($p = 0.41$), and culmen ($p = 0.39$). In general, most of the birds captured in Kenai Fjords were either in basic plumage or just beginning the molt into breeding plumage. Most of the birds showed little or no development of the brood patch at the time of capture.

There were 47 relocations recorded on the surveys and every bird was relocated at least once (fig. 11). No bird was located farther than 10 km from its capture site. Two of the radio-marked birds were confirmed depredated and their transmitters were recovered with remains of feathers. A third bird was tracked to an eagle nest and presumed depredated but the transmitter was not recovered. Bird 06-004 was tracked to a location on land on May 30, and relocated at the same location on June 1 and June 7. This bird was not located on any other survey after June 7 and its fate is unknown.

Marine Habitat

Oceanography

Water column profiles showed spatial and temporal differences in temperature and salinity between glacial and distal areas in both fjords (fig. 12). Temperature and salinity profiles demonstrated the importance of marine sills in the exchange of inner and outer fjord waters. The cool, low-salinity waters pooled behind the sills in the inner fjord, and warmer, more saline water was held outside of the sills. The sill in Northwestern Lagoon is shallower and the passage is more constricted than in Aialik Bay. Surface freshening in Northwestern Lagoon extended deeper into the water column than in Aialik Bay during all sampling periods of the study.

Chlorophyll *a* concentrations, used here as a proxy for phytoplankton standing crop, were lowest in both fjords during June 2007 (fig. 13). In general, chlorophyll *a* concentrations were consistently higher in Northwestern Lagoon compared to Aialik Bay, particularly in August 2007. Low photic depth near the glaciers corresponded with low chlorophyll *a* concentrations.

Surface water clarity was lowest near tidewater glaciers, and decreased between June and July 2008 (fig. 14). In July, low water clarity over the upper 50 m of the water column less than 3 km from Aialik Glacier indicated increased glacial runoff. Beam transmission in the upper 3 m of the water column at stations within 3 km of tidewater glaciers was on average ($\pm$ SE) 54.61 ± 9.58 percent in June, and 28.36 ± 6.76 percent in July. In contrast, average ($\pm$ SE) beam transmission below 3 m depth at stations within 3 km of a tidewater glacier was 87.52 ± 0.94 percent in June and 79.54 ± 5.16 percent in July. The median depth of 80 percent water clarity occurred at 5 and 6.5 m in June and July, respectively, for Aialik Bay stations, and at 9 m in both June and July in Northwestern Lagoon. Two stations sampled within 1 km from Aialik Glacier in July had low water clarity throughout the water column, with maximum water clarity of 73.46 percent at 99 m, and 66.6 percent at 88 m (fig. 15).

In 2008, average dissolved inorganic nitrogen (DIN) concentrations generally decreased throughout the summer and were higher in glacial areas than distal areas (table 8). Fourth root-transformed DIN differed between glacial and distal areas, and among months, but did not differ significantly between fjords (3-way ANOVA: $F_{[3, 21]} = 4.15$, $R^2 = 0.45$, $p < 0.05$). DIN was significantly higher in June than July and August, but July and August were not significantly different from one another (Tukey HSD, $\alpha = 0.05$). Average ($\pm$ SE) DIN to phosphate ratios were 2.70 ± 0.58 µM at the surface and 4.30 ± 0.57 µM at 10 m depth and were well below the Redfield ratio of 16:1 (Redfield, 1958) during all sample periods. Surface values of $Si(OH)_4$ were lowest in Aialik Bay in July and in Northwestern Lagoon in August (fig. 15).

Ammonium concentrations in the surface waters differed within and between fjords. In July 2007, ammonium concentrations were significantly different between glacial and distal stations, but not between Northwestern Lagoon and Aialik Bay (2-way ANOVA: $F_{[2,19]} = 5.45$, $R^2 = 0.36$, $p < 0.05$). In 2008, fourth root-transformed ammonium concentrations were higher at glacial stations compared to distal stations, and also in Northwestern Lagoon compared to Aialik Bay (3-way ANOVA: $F_{[4,17]} = 3.48$, $R^2 = 0.45$, $p < 0.05$). Ammonium concentrations in June were higher than July and August, whereas ammonium concentrations in July and August were not significantly different from one another (Tukey HSD, $\alpha = 0.05$).

Current measurements at the marine sills in Aialik and Northwestern Lagoons were characterized by high velocities and complex flow. The horizontal and vertical contraction of the fjord geometry accelerated the tidal currents over the sill and induced three-dimensional currents. The maximum tidal discharge measured was 12,300 m^3/s at the marine sill in Aialik Bay during the peak flood tide on August 15, 2007. The maximum tidal discharge measured at the marine sill in Northwestern Lagoon was 10,100 m^3/s during the peak ebb tide on August 15, 2007. The maximum measured velocity of 1.8 m/s was during this measurement.

In contrast, current measurements made near the front of Aialik and Northwestern Glaciers were characterized by low velocity and stratification from freshwater input. Average velocities in front of Aialik Glacier were less than 0.01 m/s. Limited data were collected in front of the Northwestern Glacier due to thick ice pack, depths in excess of the instrument's range, and limited satellite coverage. Inflow from the glaciers was not distinguishable in the velocity data, but a freshwater lens was definable in both the salinity and ADCP measurements of acoustical backscatter data (fig. 16). The sediment laden freshwater discharge from Aialik Glacier had a higher acoustical backscatter than denser water below the pycnocline. High acoustical backscatter, a proxy for turbidity, was strongest in the upper 5 m of the water column, particularly on the southern end of Aialik Glacier, which was grounded at low tide. Deeper acoustical backscatter near the northern end of the Aialik Glacier face suggested subsurface freshwater flow.

The current datasets from both Aialik Bay and Northwestern Lagoon sills indicated sediment transport along the ocean floor during flood and ebb tides. The measurements along both sills showed a discrepancy between the ADCP ship track and the GPS ship track indicating that sediment was being transported along the ocean floor at the time of the measurements. The divergence of tracks was the result of a bias in the ADCP data that was introduced when sediment particles were moving on the bed. The ADCP algorithms interpret the movement of the sediment as movement of the ADCP. The GPS data are not affected by this phenomenon and therefore represent a more accurate ship track. Sediment transport was detected at both the Aialik and Northwestern sills at peak flow. These large discharges and high velocities measured at the marine sills act to mix fresh water from the upper fjords with waters from the Gulf of Alaska.

Prey Availability

At least 28 species of fish were captured with an IKMT in 2007 and 2008 (table 9), including species important in murrelet diets such as capelin, Pacific herring, and Pacific sand lance. Saffron cod (*Eleginus gracilis*) was the most abundant species of gadid. Pacific cod (*Gadus macrocephalus*) and walleye pollock (*Theragra chalcogramma*) also were present. Mesopelagic fishes included lanternfish (Myctophidae) and northern smoothtongue (*Leuroglossus schmidti*). At least 52 species of zooplankton also were collected in 2007 and 2008 (appendixes 4–5).

At least five species of euphausiid were collected in Kenai Fjords, including (in order of abundance) *Thysanoessa inermis*, *T. raschii*, *Euphausia pacifica*, *T. spinifera*, and *T. longipes*. In 2007, trawl-caught euphausiid density was negatively associated with distance to tidewater glaciers (Spearman ρ = -0.63, p < 0.01). In 2008, the relationship between euphausiid density and glacial distance was not significantly correlated (Spearman ρ_{June} = -0.64, p = 0.12, p_{July} = 0.74, p_{August} = 0.49).

Trawl catch community structure at glacial and distal stations were not significantly different from one another (Pseudo $F_{[1,12]}$ = 1.35, p = 0.22) (table 10). There was a significant difference between fjords (Pseudo $F_{[1, 12]}$ = 2.40, p = 0.03) and also between months (Pseudo $F_{[1, 12]}$ = 7.25, p = 0.003). *Eucalanus bungii* was consistently more abundant in Aialik Bay and contributed most to dissimilarities in community structure between fjords. *Centropages abdominalis* and amphipods were more abundant in Northwestern Lagoon, contributing to 17.7 percent of the dissimilarity between fjords. Capelin larvae also were more abundant in Northwestern Lagoon than Aialik Bay and contributed to 8.0 percent of the dissimilarity between fjords. Capelin larvae were most abundant in July and contributed to 13.7 percent of the dissimilarity between July and August. Age-0 gadids were most abundant in June and contributed to 8.6 percent of the dissimilarity between June and July, and 16.5 percent of dissimilarity between June and August. Euphausiids were most abundant in July, and accounted for 6.4 percent of dissimilarities between June and July, and 8.1 percent of dissimilarities between July and August. Gelatinous zooplankton comprised the lowest proportion of the catch in proximity to tidewater glaciers, and a high proportion of the catch at distal stations (fig. 17).

Hydroacoustic measurements of schooling fish suggested within and between fjord differences over the course of the summer in 2008 (figs. 18-19). Dense forage fish aggregations were scarce in Northwestern Lagoon during June whereas abundance was highest in July and an intermediate in August. Fish aggregations in Aialik Bay were most abundant in distal areas in June and in glacial areas by August. Aialik Bay's northeastern shore in August had more numerous schools of greater magnitude than any other area during the summer. Mean (± SE) depth of schools was 39.0 ± 6.7 m in June, 46.7 ± 7.4 m in July, and 32.2 ± 3.4 m in August.

Weaker scattering nekton, including zooplankton and more dispersed fish also showed seasonal variability (fig. 18). Acoustic biomass increased throughout the summer in both fjords. Higher intensity scattering generally was associated with nearshore areas, marine sills, and tidewater glaciers. Net sampling indicated that acoustic biomass in glacial areas primarily was due to zooplankton and loose aggregations of fish. In August, weaker scattering organisms were abundant in glacial areas of both fjords.

Acoustic biomass within the upper 40 m of the water column differed significantly by month and fjord (2-way ANOVA: $F_{[3,72]} = 6.28$, $R^2 = 0.21$, $p < 0.001$). Biomass was lower in June than in July and August, but July and August were not significantly different from each other (Tukey HSD, $\alpha = 0.05$). Biomass in Aialik Bay was significantly higher than in Northwestern Lagoon (Student's t, $\alpha = 0.05$). The relationship between acoustic biomass and glacial distance differed by fjord and month (fig. 19). In Northwestern Lagoon, acoustic biomass was negatively associated with distance to glacier in June ($R^2 = 0.43$, $p < 0.05$) and July ($R^2 = 0.35$, $p < 0.05$). In Aialik Bay, acoustic biomass was positively associated with distance to glacier in June ($R^2 = 0.55$, $p < 0.01$), but this pattern did not persist through the summer.

We conducted a total of 13 beach seine sets at six sites in 2007 and 2 beach seine sets at two sites in 2008. At least 21 species of fish were collected in beach seines (table 11). Pacific sand lance (n = 1,757), pink salmon (*Oncorhynchus gorbuscha*, n = 636), and Pacific herring (n = 155) were most abundant and all three species occurred in 31 percent of beach seine sets. Pacific sand lance were consistently collected at the marine sill in McCarty Fjord and in Northwestern Lagoon. Juvenile Pacific herring were collected near the head of Aialik Bay in Northwestern Lagoon, Pederson Lagoon, and Verdant Cove. Surf melt (*Hypomesus pretiosus*, n = 62) also were among the more common species, and were caught at the marine sill in McCarty Fjord, Pederson Lagoon, and Northwestern Lagoon. A single capelin in spawning condition (spent female) was collected in Pederson lagoon on August 3, 2007.

Fish observed in Kittlitz's and marbled murrelet bills were juvenile Pacific herring (n = 15), Pacific sand lance (n = 2), surf smelt (n = 1), and capelin (n = 1). The approximate size of herring in bill loads was 95–110 mm, and one sand lance bill load was estimated at 110 mm in length. Kittlitz's Murrelets were observed eating (that is, surfacing with fish and swallowing them) herring and sand lance near areas where those species were collected in beach seines.

Habitat Model

Habitat preferences differed between Kittlitz's and marbled murrelets (table 12), despite their apparent distributional overlap in Kenai Fjords. Where ice was present, the best model showed Kittlitz's murrelets had a higher probability of occurrence in Aialik Bay, over deeper water, closer to the tidewater glaciers, and where acoustic biomass was higher. The probability of marbled murrelet occurrence was negatively related to bottom depth and ice cover. The most parsimonious models resulted from the 400-m scale for the Kittlitz's murrelet and 800-m scale for the marbled murrelet. A smaller segment size resulted in the best model for Kittlitz's murrelets because data were restricted to observations where ice was present, and greater segment sizes resulted in sample sizes that were too low to draw meaningful inference.

Discussion

In this section, we first discuss our rationale for survey design including the treatment of flying birds, transect methodology, and timing of surveys. We then consider the effects of variability in bird distribution over space and time on population estimates for Kenai Fjords. Finally, we discuss the overall findings from telemetry, productivity surveys, and marine habitat characterization efforts.

Survey Design

In 2006–08, a new sampling regime was designed to standardize the study design and make the survey easier to replicate in the future. Changes from an earlier survey included orienting the offshore transects along latitude lines and creating a new set of systematically selected coastal transects to ensure that proper coverage was afforded to the entire coastline. This change in transect location may cause issues with direct comparability among years; however, we intended for the 2006–08 transects to systematically cover the areas where murrelets are most likely to occur while also maximizing repeatability.

Other considerations for survey design include the treatment of flying birds, survey methodology, and timing of surveys. The inclusion of flying birds in population analyses overestimates density because the targets move faster than the ship and more birds fly over the survey area than are present at one instant in time (Tasker and others, 1984). Therefore, the inclusion of flying birds can present a problem for density calculations and population estimates if their numbers represent a significant portion of the overall total. Excluding flying birds altogether from population analyses, however, underestimates the number of birds in the area. During this study, flying birds generally made up about 5 percent or less of Kittlitz's and marbled murrelet observations, with the exception of the mid-season surveys in 2006 when flying birds made up nearly 20 percent of Kittlitz's murrelet observations (table 4). Another issue is that a large proportion of flying birds was comprised of unidentified *Brachyramphus* murrelets (table 4). To address these issues, we presented an adjusted total population estimate that includes line transect estimates for birds on the water and strip transect estimates for flying birds for Kittlitz's, marbled, and all *Brachyramphus* murrelets (table 3).

A combination of strip and line transect methodology was used to more accurately estimate population size for *Brachyramphus* murrelets. Strip transects underestimate marine bird population size when observers are unable to detect every bird within the strip (Buckland and others, 1993; 2001), for example, if sighting probability decreases with distance from the survey vessel. Line transect methodology incorporates detection probability based on perpendicular distance of detected birds to the transect line, essentially creating a correction factor for undetected birds. Detection probabilities in some but not all stratum-year combinations decreased with distance from the vessel. Weather conditions in 2006 contributed to a lower sighting probability of murrelets with distance from the ship track on the more exposed outer coast and offshore transects. In most strata-year combinations, however, detection of *Brachyramphus* murrelets was equal to one across the strip width. The combined strip and line transect methodology for counting murrelets probably is a logistically reasonable way to achieve more accurate population estimates than strip transects alone, despite the need for a high level of observer training and constant reinforcement of distance calibration.

When deciding the best time to survey seabird populations for status and trend analysis, managers are faced with decisions regarding the tradeoff between statistical significance and biological significance, as these are rarely the same (Hatch, 2003). The ability to detect a statistically significant trend is strongly dependent on the number and precision of samples (Gerrodette, 1987), and so with a reasonable number of samples, the best time to survey birds to detect trend is when numbers at sea exhibit the lowest variability. However, a more reasonable approach may be to survey at a more biologically significant time (Seavy and Reynolds, 2007), for example, when peak numbers of birds are observed at sea to estimate total numbers at sea. The trade-off between conducting surveys during timing of lowest variability (early-season, when one of the pair is usually sitting on the nest) and timing of maximum density (mid-season, when both birds of the pair are actively foraging to feed the chick, and when subadults/non-breeders occur) is substantial and can have important consequences for population estimates and trend analysis. For murrelets, interannual and within-season variability is high, and so it would be best to conduct multiple surveys within a single year (Becker and others, 1999). Timing of highest densities on the water (mid-season for Kittlitz's murrelets, late season for marbled murrelets) did not correspond with the timing of lowest variability (usually early season, late May–early June) for murrelets in Kenai Fjords during this study, and this concurs with seasonal patterns observed in other studies (Speckman and others, 2000; Romano and others, 2004). Historical survey effort for population estimation in Kenai Fjords occurred from June 19 to July 14 (Van Pelt and Piatt, 2003) and our mid-season surveys are comparable with these historical surveys. The data indicate that the best trend information, however, would come from early season surveys (late May–early June) for Kittlitz's murrelets, and from mid-season surveys (late June–early July) for marbled murrelets.

Population and Distribution

Based on an average of point estimates for mid-season coastwide surveys in Kenai Fjords, the estimated population ($\pm$ SE) of Kittlitz's murrelets was 670 ($\pm$ 144) individuals, and marbled murrelets was 5,855 ($\pm$ 1,163) individuals. The most recent information suggests that this is perhaps 3 percent of Kittlitz's and 2 percent of marbled murrelet Alaska-wide populations (Piatt and others, 2007; U.S. Fish and Wildlife Service, 2008). During this study, Kittlitz's murrelets largely were restricted to the areas closest to tidewater glaciers, and nearly always found above the sills in McCarty Fjord, Northwestern Lagoon, and Aialik Bay. Marbled murrelets were more widely distributed, occurring in both glacial and distal areas of the fjords, and also in the more exposed outer coast areas. Although their distribution in the upper fjords overlapped, the two species generally utilized different habitats (figs. 8–9).

Interannual variability in murrelet abundance was high, and these short-term fluctuations in the abundance of Kittlitz's murrelets may have simply reflected regional abundance patterns that were concordant with surveys in Kachemak Bay (Kuletz and others, 2008) and Icy Bay (Michelle Kissling, U.S. Fish and Wildlife Service, oral. commun., 2008). An influx of Kittlitz's murrelets into Kenai Fjords during 2006 also was noted in nearby Kachemak Bay, whereas abundance was down in all three areas in 2007 compared to other years. The influx of Kittlitz's murrelets in Kachemak Bay during 2006 was confined to the outer bay survey area and birds may have come from lower Cook Inlet populations (Kuletz and others, 2008). In Kenai Fjords, Kittlitz's and marbled murrelets exhibited similar fluctuations in abundance between years, suggesting that interannual variability resulted from a common cause for both species. Because 2007 was an anomalous year for oceanographic conditions in the Gulf of Alaska (Janout and others, 2010), it is possible that regional oceanography played a role in low abundance of murrelets during mid-season surveys during that year. The ultimate cause of this variability is unknown, but may possibly arise from fluctuations in breeding effort (when many birds do not breed and remain offshore), pulses of recruiting birds from previously successful years of reproduction, or pulses of sub-adult birds prospecting near breeding grounds (see below).

Within-season density patterns differed by species. When monthly densities were averaged over the three years of the study, Kittlitz's murrelets increased in density from June to July, followed by a decline in density by early to mid-August. For marbled murrelets, average densities increased slowly from June to July and increased dramatically by late season counts in early to mid August. This suggests that post breeding dispersal occurred earlier in the season for Kittlitz's murrelets, and presumably began by mid July. For marbled murrelets, abundance was highest in August and similar to late season density peaks in other areas (Speckman and others, 2000; Romano and others, 2004). Late season increases in marbled murrelets were likely due to variable subadult attendance and may be related to the strength of subadult cohorts and food availability (Speckman and others, 2000).

Telemetry

A likely Kittlitz's murrelet nest was located in Northwestern Lagoon during 2006 by radio telemetry. The signal was located in an area that would be difficult (though not impossible) to reach due to cliffs and the persistence of snow blocking the route early in the season. The site where the signal was tracked had large, snow free patches on May 30 (N 59.77063°; W 149.89635°). Relocation effort of radio-tagged birds suggest Kittlitz's murrelets showed high site fidelity within Kenai Fjords; all birds were relocated within 10 km of their capture location in the upper fjord areas of Aialik Bay and Northwestern Lagoon. This is comparable to relocation distance for tagged Kittlitz's murrelets in Glacier Bay (Romano and others, 2007b) and satellite tagged birds in Icy Bay and Kachemak Bay (J. Piatt, unpublished data, 2009).

Productivity

Very few fledgling *Brachyramphus* murrelets, particularly Kittlitz's murrelets, were observed over the course of this study despite our effort to survey during what should have been the peak fledging period in south-central Alaska (Kuletz and Piatt, 1999; Kuletz and others, 2008). Similar efforts in Prince William Sound and Glacier Bay also were unsuccessful in finding many juvenile Kittlitz's murrelets at sea (Day and Nigro, 2004, M. Romano, U.S. Geological Survey, oral commun., 2007). In contrast, the number of Kittlitz's murrelet juveniles peaked in Kachemak Bay during mid-August and rapidly declined shortly thereafter (Kuletz and others, 2008). The low number of juvenile Kittlitz's murrelets sighted in Kenai Fjords may indicate low breeding success and productivity during the course of this study. Alternatively, the absence of Kittlitz's murrelets during August surveys may reflect the possibility that Kittlitz's murrelet fledglings leave the coastal area immediately and that the timing of our coastal surveys provided a very short window of opportunity for sighting.

We have no way of knowing how many non-breeding adults were present during productivity surveys, and these numbers would tend to deflate estimates of productivity. Low productivity indices also may reflect survey effort that missed the peak fledging period, particularly in 2007, when we observed an apparently late spring bloom and late fledgling period as suggested by the high number of birds holding fish (an indication of chick rearing) during mid-August surveys.

Habitat

Oceanography

Meso-scale (25 km in this study) patterns of phytoplankton production may influence interannual variability in local attendance of murrelets at sea, and this may explain the high interannual variability in mid-season counts. Within-season variability in Kittlitz's murrelet density differed in 2007 compared to other years. The highest density of Kittlitz's murrelets occurred late in 2007, which suggests a delay in the onset of breeding during that year. Sampling along the Gulf of Alaska shelf adjacent to Kenai Fjords suggests 2007 was an anomalous year (Janout and others, 2010). Spring and summer temperature and salinity profiles fell outside the long-term average standard deviations in May, with cooler temperatures throughout the water column, fresher water at depth, and more saline water near the surface (Janout and others, 2010.

Seasonal fluctuations in chlorophyll *a* and nutrient dynamics during summer 2008 suggest that the mechanisms governing these ecosystem components differ between fjords. Low chlorophyll *a* concentrations in glacial areas compared to distal areas of Aialik Bay indicated that chlorophyll *a* production in glacial areas is more influenced by shelf waters, which likely is because of the orientation of the mouth of Aialik Bay relative to the Alaska Coastal Current. Chlorophyll *a* patterns were more consistent and sustained in Northwestern Lagoon throughout the 2008 summer, with relatively high chlorophyll *a* concentrations in glacial areas in June and July. Northwestern Lagoon is more enclosed with a more narrow passage and shallow sill, which inhibits exchange with more oceanic waters in distal areas (Gay and Armato, 1999). Our results in Northwestern Lagoon are in accordance with similar findings in Glacier Bay, Alaska, another enclosed and silled fjord that experiences high and sustained chlorophyll *a* concentrations, particularly in areas of intermediate stratification (Etherington and others, 2007).

Our data were in accordance with the hypothesis that a water clarity profile characterized by high turbidity near the surface and clearer water below is important to Kittlitz's murrelets feeding in glacial-marine environments (Kuletz and others, 2008). Low water clarity as a result of glacial runoff in Kenai Fjords generally was constrained to the surface layer (5–9 m) near tidewater glaciers. The water column below the turbid freshwater lens was clearer, and this physical feature is common in Kittlitz's murrelet foraging habitat elsewhere (Barron and Barron, 2005; Kuletz and others, 2008). Low water clarity was detected throughout the water column near Aialik Glacier in July, however, indicating higher subsurface sediment outflow as glacial melt increased throughout the summer warming period. This effect was very localized (less than 1 km from glacier) as subsurface beam transmission reached 80 percent at 12-m depth at a station sampled 2.3 km from the glacier.

Prey Availability

The near-surface availability of euphausiids in the turbid waters near glacial stream outflows provided a prey resource for Kittlitz's murrelets, and may have influenced their at-sea distribution. Euphausiids are an important prey type in Kittlitz's murrelet diets (Sanger, 1987; Hobson and others, 1994; Day and others, 1999), comprising as much as 44 percent of Kittlitz's murrelet and 31 percent of marbled murrelet diets in Alaska (Hobson and others, 1994). Weslawski and others (2000), who also found euphausiids were most abundant in the surface waters near glaciers, suggest that macrozooplankton are entrapped in inner fjord basins by physical processes, such as estuarine circulation. In addition to physical processes, euphausiid distribution is maintained by behavior, in particular, diel migration in response to light and also their relatively strong swimming abilities (Zhou and others, 2005).

Although there are several explanations for the occurrence of euphausiids in surface waters near glaciers, including reproductive behavior, net avoidance in clear water, or subsurface upwelling, we believe that once entrained into glacial areas, near surface euphausiids were likely influenced by turbid glacial outflow that inhibited a photic cue for diel vertical migration. Euphausiids swarm to reproduce in surface waters during daylight hours (Hanamura and others, 1989) and timing of surveys in Kenai Fjords overlapped with the reproductive period of euphausiids in nearby Prince William Sound and along the Gulf of Alaska Shelf (Pinchuk and others, 2008). However, the most abundant species collected within Kenai Fjords was *T. inermis*, which usually reproduces between April and May (Pinchuk and others, 2008) and earlier than our sampling commenced. Euphausiids collected in Northwestern Lagoon in July 2007 (this study) had spawned previously but were not actively reproducing at the time of capture (samples verified by A. Pinchuk, University of Alaska Fairbanks). Alternatively, it is possible that net avoidance in clear water explains the higher abundance of euphausiid catches in turbid water (Ken Coyle, University of Alaska Fairbanks, oral commun., 2008). We believe this was not the case, however, because trawl catches in Glacier Bay, using a net large enough (mouth opening of 50 m^2) to rule out net avoidance by organisms as small as euphausiids, showed a similar pattern of high daytime euphausiid abundance in surface waters nearest the glaciers (Robards and others, 2003).

Subsurface glacial outflow can cause local upwelling, or "brown zones," near the face of tidewater glaciers that bring biomass to the surface and can be an important physical structuring mechanism for zooplankton (Hartley and Dunbar, 1938); however, some tidewater glaciers in Kenai Fjords were grounded at low tide during this study. Observations of tidal velocity do not support the hypothesis that zooplankton are brought to the surface by upwelling because of subsurface freshwater flow from tidewater glaciers in Kenai Fjords, although this may be the case in other fjords (Day and others, 2003). Vertical velocities were not distinguishable in the current measurements from the front of the Aialik Glacier face because of the low overall current velocities relative to boat speed. In contrast, vertical velocities indicating upwelling and complex currents were detected in ADCP cross sections made at the sills. This is a key structural feature that induces mixing of inner fjord waters with Gulf of Alaska waters, and is a possible mechanism for bringing macrozooplankton into glacial areas (Carpenter, 1983).

Other marine organisms that typically occur at deeper depths during the day have been documented in surface waters near glaciers. Carpenter (1983) found that shrimp and other zooplankton were abundant throughout the water column near the face of Aialik Glacier; however, these crustaceans were collected only in deeper water during the day at the marine sill just 10 km away. This vertical distribution of shrimp near the glacier face was attributed to reduced light conditions due to turbid glacial outflow. Abookire and others (2002) also speculated that low light conditions explained the daytime presence of mesopelagic fishes in the turbid surface waters in Glacier Bay. Our data, along with similar observations of other studies, lend support to the hypothesis that the daytime, near-surface occurrence of marine organisms that typically undergo diel migrations may be because of the lack of a photic cue beneath turbid glacial outflows.

Monthly acoustic biomass measurements in Kenai Fjords during 2008 indicated lower prey availability in June compared to later in the summer, and this was most likely a lagged response to marine production in the fjords. Patterns of acoustic biomass differed between fjords, with biomass in Northwestern Lagoon generally decreasing with distance from tidewater glaciers throughout the summer. Higher abundance of weak-scattering organisms, such as zooplankton in the upper 40 m near the head of Northwestern Lagoon, was a driver of this relationship. The relationship between acoustic biomass and glacial distance in Aialik Bay was more variable over the summer, with a significant positive response in the early season, and no significant relationship later in the season. In the middle and late summer, however, dense forage fish schools had clearly moved into glacial areas of Aialik Bay (fig. 19), a pattern that is consistent with studies elsewhere (Robards and others, 1999). These observations suggest forage fish abundance lags the peak in lower trophic level production.

Nearshore habitats provide food resources, cover, and nursery habitat for forage fishes, and beach seining has proven an efficient way to sample fishes important in murrelet diets in these areas (Johnson and Thedinga, 2005). We documented the occurrence of important murrelet forage species including Pacific herring, Pacific sand lance, capelin, and surf smelt with beach seines in 2007 and 2008. We also observed a large group of Kittlitz's murrelets feeding (capturing and swallowing at the surface) on Pacific sand lance adjacent to a large kelp bed near the McCarty Glacier sill in the East Arm of Nuka Bay, where sand lance were frequently caught in beach seines.

Glacial fjords in Alaska provide important spawning habitat and nursery areas for capelin during the spring and summer (Brown, 2002; Arimitsu and others, 2008). In Glacier Bay, a glacial fjord in southeast Alaska, the spawn timing for capelin was protracted, with spatial and temporal variation in maturation of ripe females (Arimitsu and others, 2008). In Kenai Fjords, spawning capelin were found in Pederson Lagoon, and larval capelin used Northwestern Lagoon as a nursery area. We found evidence that the capelin spawning period was synchronous in Kenai Fjords during 2008. Larval capelin were an order of magnitude more abundant in trawl catches during July than they were in June and August, and there was little variation in length frequency (table 9). This suggests that capelin spawning dynamics in Kenai Fjords differed from Glacier Bay, and also suggests that capelin can provide predictable forage resources for murrelets and other piscivorous marine birds in Kenai Fjords.

Concurrent hydroacoustic and bird survey data indicated that Kittlitz's murrelets utilized lower density forage fish aggregations and zooplankton that occur in the turbid glacial plume near tidewater glaciers. Low-density and dispersed prey was characteristic of prey availability for murrelets and other seabirds also in Prince William Sound (Ostrand and others, 1998, 2004). Although dense forage fish schools moved into the inner fjords by August 2008, earlier in the season, the area closest to tidewater glaciers contained weak-scattering organisms, such as zooplankton and low-density fish schools. Higher turbidity near glaciers may sustain low density or dispersed prey because (1) the lack of a photic cue inhibits vertical migration for zooplankton and fish, and (2) visual cues that aid in dense schooling behavior are suppressed in very turbid water (Partridge and Pitcher, 1980).

In Kenai Fjords, interannual variability in murrelet population estimates was high, and marine habitat preferences differed by species. Low population estimates were coincident with anomalous marine conditions in 2007, which may reflect the influence of meso-scale oceanographic conditions on the timing of nesting phenology (inferred from at-sea density). As in previous studies (Day and Nigro, 2000; Day and others, 2000), Kittlitz's murrelets were strongly associated with marine conditions found in waters adjacent to tidewater glaciers. This habitat was characterized by cool, sediment-laden glacial melt water where low light penetration limits phytoplankton abundance but also may enhance the availability of suitable prey near the surface. Dense forage fish schools moved into glacial areas over the course of the summer. In contrast, marbled murrelets were more associated with shallow water and tended to avoid ice in glacial areas, and they apparently had a wider tolerance to the range of marine habitat characteristics found within Kenai Fjords National Park.

Acknowledgments

This project was funded by the U.S. Geological Survey, including funds from the Alaska Science Center, and funds from the Natural Resource Protection Program, which is dedicated to research needs of the National Park Service. Funding to help support the late-season surveys for fledglings was provided by the Alaska Coastal Marine Resources Grant Program of the National Park Foundation. This project would not have been possible without the support of Naomi Bargmann, Camille Castaneda, Karl Deutsch, Gary Drew, Gavin McMorrow, Stuart Meyers, Aileen Miller, Andrew Ramey, Julie Schram, Greg Snedgen, Indu Soini, Shiway Wang, and Jon Wetzel. The staff of Kenai Fjords National Park, including Shelley Hall, Mark Kansteiner, Meg Hahr, Caroline Jezierski, Dan Shultz, and the captain and crew of the M/V *Serac* provided valuable assistance and support to this project. Chris Stark (UAF) analyzed zooplankton samples, and Kathy Krogslund (UW) analyzed nutrients samples. We also thank Bill Thompson (NPS), Deb Nigro (BLM), Dan Mulcahy (USGS), Kathy Kuletz (USFWS) Nicola Hillgruber (UAF), Terry Quinn (UAF), Franz Mueter (UAF), and Chris Hay-Jahans (UAS), who provided assistance during the planning and analysis phases of the study.

References Cited

Abookire, A.A., Piatt, J.F., and Speckman, S.G., 2002, A nearsurface, daytime occurrence of two mesopelagic fish species (Stenobrachius leucopsarus and Leuroglossus schmidti) in a glacial fjord: Fisheries Bulletin, v. 100, p. 376–380.

Agler, B.A., Kendall, S.J., and Irons, D.B., 1998, Abundance and distribution of Marbled and Kittlitz's Murrelets in Southcentral and Southeast Alaska: The Condor, v. 100, p. 254–265.

Arimitsu, M.L., Piatt, J.F., Litzow, M.A., Abookire, A.A., Romano, M.D., and Robards, M.D., 2008, Distribution and spawning dynamics of capelin (Mallotus villosus) in Glacier Bay, Alaska: a cold water refugium; Fisheries: Oceanography, v. 17, no. 2, p. 137–146.

Barron, M.G., and Barron, K.J., 2005, Glacial influences on solar radiation in a subarctic sea: Photochemistry and Photobiology, v. 81, p. 187–189.

Becker, B.H., Beissinger, S.R., and Carter, H.R., 1999, At-sea density monitoring of marbled murrelets in central California: methodological considerations: The Condor, v. 99, p. 743–755.

Bradley, R.W., Cooke, F., Lougheed, L.W., and Boyd, W.S., 2004, Inferring breeding success through radio telemetry in the marbled murrelet: Journal of Wildlife Management, v. 68, p. 318–331.

Brown, E.D., 2002, Life history, distribution, and size structure of Pacific capelin in Prince William Sound and the northern Gulf of Alaska: ICES J. Mar. Sci., v. 59, p. 983–996.

Buckland, S.T., Anderson, D.R., Burnham, K.P., and Laake, J.L., 1993, Estimating Abundance of Biological Populations: London, Chapman and Hall, 446 p.

Buckland, S.T., Anderson, D.R., Burnham, K.P., Laake, J.L., Borchers, D.L., and Thomas, L.T., 2001, Introduction to Distance Sampling: New York, Oxford University Press, 432 p.

Carpenter, T.A., 1983, Pandalid shrimps in a tidewater-glacier fjord, Aialik Bay, Alaska, University of Alaska Fairbanks, MSc. Thesis, 132 p.

Day, R.H., Kuletz, K.J., and Nigro, D.A., 1999, Kittlitz's Murrelet (Brachyramphus brevirostris), in Poole, A., and Gill, F., eds., The Birds of North America, No. 435: Philadelphia, PA, The Birds of North America, Inc., p. 28.

Day, R.H., and Nigro, D.A., 2000, Feeding ecology of Kittlitz's and marbled murrelets in Prince William Sound, Alaska: Waterbirds, v. 23, p. 1–14.

Day, R.H., and Nigro, D.A., 2004, Is the Kittlitz's Murrelet Exhibiting Reproductive Problems in Prince William Sound, Alaska?: Waterbirds, v. 27, p. 89–95.

Day, R.H., Nigro, D.A., and Prichard, A.K., 2000, At-sea habitat use by the Kittlitz's murrelet (Brachyramphus brevirostris) in nearshore waters of Prince William Sound, Alaska: Marine Ornithology, v. 28, p. 105–114.

Day, R.H., Prichard, A.K., and Nigro, D.A., 2003, Ecological specialization and overlap of Brachyramphus murrelets in Prince William Sound, Alaska: Auk, v. 120, p. 680–699.

Dormann, C.F., McPherson, J.M., Araujo, M.B., Bivand, R., Bollinger, J., Carl, G., Davies, R.G., Hirzel, A., Jetz, W., Kissling, D., Kuhn, I., Ohlemuller, R., Peres-Neto, P.R., Reineking, B., Schroder, B., Schurr, F.M., and Wilson, R., 2007, Methods to account for spatial autocorrelation in the analysis of species distributional data: a review: Ecography, v. 30, p. 609–628.

Drew, G.S., and Piatt, J.F., 2008, Using geographic information systems to compare non-uniform marine bird surveys: detecting the decline of Kittlitz's Murrelet (Brachyramphus brevirostris) in Glacier Bay, Alaska: The Auk, v. 125, no. 1, p. 178–182.

Efron, B., and Tibshirani, R., 1986, Bootstrap methods for standard errors, confidence intervals, and other measures of statistical accuracy: Statistical Science, v. 1, no. 1, p. 54–75.

Etherington, L.L., Hooge, P.N., Hooge, E.R., and Hill, D.F., 2007, Oceanography of Glacier Bay, Alaska: Implications for biological patterns in a glacial fjord estuary: Estuaries and Coasts, v. 30, no. 6, p. 927–944.

Foote, K.G., Knudsen, H.P., Vestnes, G., MacLennan, D.N., and Simmonds, E.J., 1987, Calibration of acoustic instruments for fish density estimation: a practical guide: ICES Cooperative Research Report 144, 57 p.

Gay, S.M., and Armato, P.J., 1999, Hydrography of McCarty Fjord, Northwestern Fjord and Aialik Bay, Kenai Fjords National Park, Alaska: Cordova, Ala., Prince William Sound Science Center, 47 p.

Gerrodette, T., 1987, A power analysis for detecting trends: Ecology, v. 68, p. 1364–1372.

Gould, P.J., and Forsell, D.J., 1989, Techniques for shipboard surveys of marine birds: U.S. Fish and Wildlife Service Technical Report 25, 22 p.

Hanamura, Y., Kotori, M., and Hamaoka, S., 1989, Daytime surface swarms of the euphausiid Thysanoessa inermis off the west coast of Hokkaido, northern Japan: Marine Biology, v. 102, p. 369–376.

Hartley, C.H., and Dunbar, M.J., 1938, On the hydrographic mechanism of the so-called brown zones associated with tidewater glaciers: Journal of Marine Research, v. 1, p. 305–311.

Hatch, S.A., 2003, Statistical power for detecting trends with applications to seabird monitoring: Biological Conservation, v. 111, p. 317–329.

Hobson, K.A., Piatt, J.F., and Pittocchelli, J., 1994, Using stable isotopes to determine seabird trophic relationships: Journal of Animal Ecology, v. 63, p. 786798.

Janout, M.A., Weingartner, T.J., Royer, T.C., and Danielson, S., 2010, On the nature of winter cooling and the recent temperature shift on the northern Gulf of Alaska shelf: Journal of Geophysical Research, v. 115, C05023, doi:10.1029/2009JC005774.

Johnson, S.W., and Thedinga, J.F., 2005, Fish use and size of eelgrass meadows in Southeastern Alaska: a baseline for long-term assessment of biotic change: Northwest Science, v. 79, p. 141–155.

Kaler, R.S., Kenney, L.A., and Sandercock, B.K., 2009, Breeding ecology of Kittlitz's murrelets at Agattu Island, Aleutian Islands, Alaska: Waterbirds, v. 32, no. 3, p. 363–479.

Kenwood, R.E., 2001, A manual for wildlife radio tagging: San Diego, Academic Press, 321 p.

Kissling, M.L., Reid, M., Lukacs, P.M., Gende, S.M., and Lewis, S.B., 2007, Understanding abundance patterns of a declining seabird: implications for monitoring: Ecological Applications, v. 17, no. 8, p. 2164–2174.

Kuletz, K.J., Labunski, E.A., and Speckman, S.G., 2008, Abundance, distribution and decadal trends of Kittlitz's and marbled murrelets and other marine species in Kachemak Bay, Alaska: U.S. Fish and Wildlife Service, Final Report to the Alaska Department of Fish and Game, Project No. 14, 119 p.

Kuletz, K.J., and Piatt, J.F., 1999, Juvenile marbled murrelet nurseries and the productivity index: The Wilson Bulletin, v. 111, no. 2, p. 257–261.

McShane, C., Hamer, T., Carter, H.R., Swartzman, G., Freisen, V., Ainley, D.G., Tressler, R., Nelson, K., Burger, A., Spear, L., Mohagen, T., Martin, R., Henkel, L., Prindle, K., Strong, C., and Keany, J., 2004, Evaluation report for the 5-year status review of the marbled murrelet in Washington, Oregon, and California: EDAW, Inc., 356 p.

Mehlum, F., Hunt, G.L., Klusek, Z., Decker, M.B., and Nordlund, N., 1996, The importance of prey aggregations to the distribution of Brunnich's guillemots in Storfjorden, Svalbard: Polar Biology, v. 16, p. 537–547.

Newman, S.H., Takekawa, J.Y., Whitworth, D.L., and Burkett, E.E., 1999, Subcutaneous anchor attachment increases retention of radio transmitters on seabirds: Xantus' and marbled murrelets: Journal of Field Ornithology, v. 70, p. 520–534.

Ostrand, W.D., Coyle, K.O., and Drew, G.S., 1998, Selection of forage fish schools by murrelets and tufted puffins in Prince William Sound, Alaska: Condor, v. 100, p. 286–297.

Ostrand, W.D., Howlin, S., and Gotthardt, T., 2004, Fish school selection by marbled murrelets in Prince William Sound, Alaska: Responses to changes in availability: Marine Ornithology, v. 32, p. 69–76.

Partridge, B.L., and Pitcher, T.J., 1980, The sensory basis of fish schools: Relative roles of lateral line and vision: Journal of Comparative Physiology v. 135, p. 315–325.

Piatt, J.F., Kuletz, K.J., Burger, A.E., Hatch, S.A., Friesen, V.L., Birt, T.P., Arimitsu, M.L., Drew, G.S., Harding, A.M.A., and Bixler, K.S., 2007, Status review of the marbled murrelet (Brachyramphus marmoratus) in Alaska and British Columbia: U.S. Geological Survey Open-File Report 2006-1387, 258 p.

Pinchuk, A.I., Coyle, K.O., and Hopcroft, R.R., 2008, Climate-related variability in abundance and reproduction of euphausiids in the northern Gulf of Alaska in 1998-2003: Progress in Oceanography, v. 77, p. 203–216.

R Development Core Team, 2008, R: A language and environment for statistical coputing. R Foundation for Statistical Computing: Vienna, Austria, R Development Core Team (Also available at *http://www.R-project.org*).

Redfield, A.C., 1958, The biological control of chemical factors in the environment: American Scientist, v. 46, p. 205–221.

Robards, M.D., Drew, G.S., Piatt, J.F., Anson, J.M., Abookire, A.A., Bodkin, J.L., Hooge, P.N., and Speckman, S.G., 2003, Ecology of selected marine communities in Glacier Bay: zooplankton, forage fish, seabirds and marine mammals: U.S. Geological Survey, Alaska Science Center, Final report to the National Park Service, 156 p.

Robards, M.D., Piatt, J.F., Kettle, A.B., and Abookire, A.A., 1999, Temporal and geographic variation in fish communities of lower Cook Inlet, Alaska: Fisheries Bulletin, v. 97, no. 4, p. 962–977.

Romano, M.D., Piatt, J.F., and Carter, H.R., 2007a, First successful radio-telemetry study of Kittlitz's murrelet—problems and potential, in The Fourth Glacier Bay Science Symposium, Juneau, Alaska, October 26-28, 2004)[Proceedings], p. 120-123.

Romano, M.D., Piatt, J.F., and Carter, H.R., 2007b, First successful radio-telemetry study of Kittlitz's murrelet - Problems and potential, in Proceedings of the Fourth Glacier Bay Science Symposium: U.S. Geological Survey Scientific Investigations Report 2007-5047, p. 120-123.

Romano, M.R., Arimitsu, M.L., Piatt, J.F., Agness, A.M., and Drew, G.S., 2004, At-sea density and distribution of Kittlitz's murrelets (Brachyramphus brevirostris) and Marbled Murrelets (Brachyramphus marmoratus) in Glacier Bay, Alaska, Summer 2003: U.S. Geological Survey Alaska Science Center, Annual report to the National Park Service, 68 p.

Romano, M.R., Piatt, J.F., and Dubuisson, C., 2006, Kittlitz's and Marbled Murrelets in Kenai Fjords National Park, Alaska: At-sea distribution and abundance, and initial observations of radio-marked Kittlitz's Murrelets: USGS Alaska Science Center, 2006 Annual Report to Kenai Fjords National Park, 47 p.

Sanger, G.A., 1987, Trophic levels and trophic relationships of seabirds in the Gulf of Alaska, in Croxall, J.P., ed., Seabirds: feeding ecology and role in marine ecosystems: Cambridge, Cambridge University Press, p. 229–257.

Seavy, N.E., and Reynolds, M.H., 2007, Is statistical power to detect trends a good assessment of population monitoring?: Biological Conservation, v. 140, p. 187–191.

Simmonds, J., and MacLennan, D.N., 2005, Fisheries Acoustics Theory and Practice: Ames, Iowa, Blackwell Science, 437 p.

Speckman, S.G., Springer, A.M., Piatt, J.F., and Thomas, D.L., 2000, Temporal variability in abundance of marbled murrelets at sea in southeast Alaska: Waterbirds, v. 23, no. 3, p. 364–377.

Strong, C., 1995, Distribution of marbled murrelets along the Oregon coast in 1992: Northwestern Naturalist, v. 76, no. 1, p. 99–105.

Tasker, M.L., Jones, P.H., Dixon, T., and Blake, B.F., 1984, Counting seabirds at sea from ships: a review of methods employed and a suggestion for a standardized approach: Auk, v. 101, p. 567–677.

Thomas, L.T., Laake, J.L., Rexstad, E., Strindberg, S., Marques, F.F.C., Buckland, S.T., Borchers, D.L., Anderson, D.R., Burnham, K.P., Burt, M.L., Hedley, S.L., Pollard, J.H., Bishop, J.R.B., and Marques, T.A., 2009, Distance 6.0. Release 2, Research Unit for Wildlife Population Assessment, University of St. Andrews, UK, website, accessed July 1, 2010 at *http://www.ruwpa.st-and.ac.uk/distance/*.

U.S. Fish and Wildlife Service, 2008, Candidate listing priority assignment for Kittlitz's murrelet: U.S. Fish and Wildlife Service, 30 p.

Van Pelt, T.I., and Piatt, J.F., 2003, Population status of Kittlitz's and Marbled Murrelets, and surveys for other marine bird and mammal species in the Kenai Fjords area, Alaska: U.S. Geological Survey Alaska Science Center, Annual Report to the U.S. Fish and Wildlife Service, 65 p.

Weslawski, J.M., Pedersen, G., Petersen, S.F., and Paorazinski, K., 2000, Entrapment of macrozooplankton in an Arctic fjord basin, Kongsfjorden, Svalbard: Oceanologia, v. 42, no. 1, p. 57–69.

Whitworth, D.L., Takekawa, J.Y., Carter, H.R., and McIver, W.R., 1997, A night-lighting technique for at-sea capture of Xantus' murrelets: Colonial Waterbirds, v. 20, p. 525–531.

Wiles, G.C., Calkin, P.E., and Post, A., 1995, Glacier fluctuations in the Kenai Fjords, Alaska, U.S.A.: An evaluation of controls on iceberg-calving glaciers: Arctic and Alpine Research, v. 27, no. 3, p. 234–245.

Zhou, M., Zhu, Y., and Tande, K.S., 2005, Circulation and behavior of euphausiids in two Norwegian sub-Arctic fjords: Marine Ecology Progress Series, v. 300, p. 159–178.

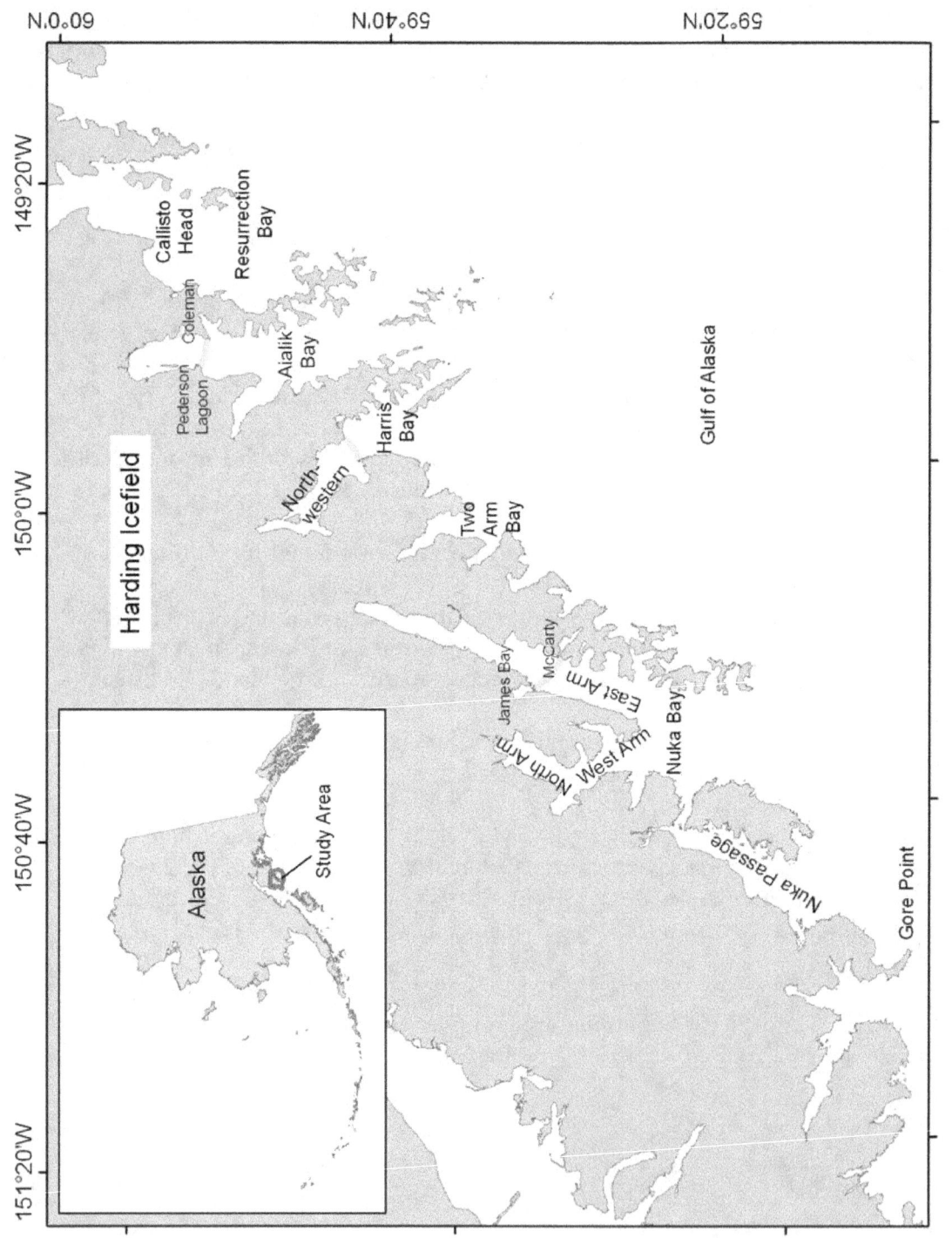

Figure 1. Map showing Kenai Fjords study area showing place names used in this report. Marine sills are shown in yellow.

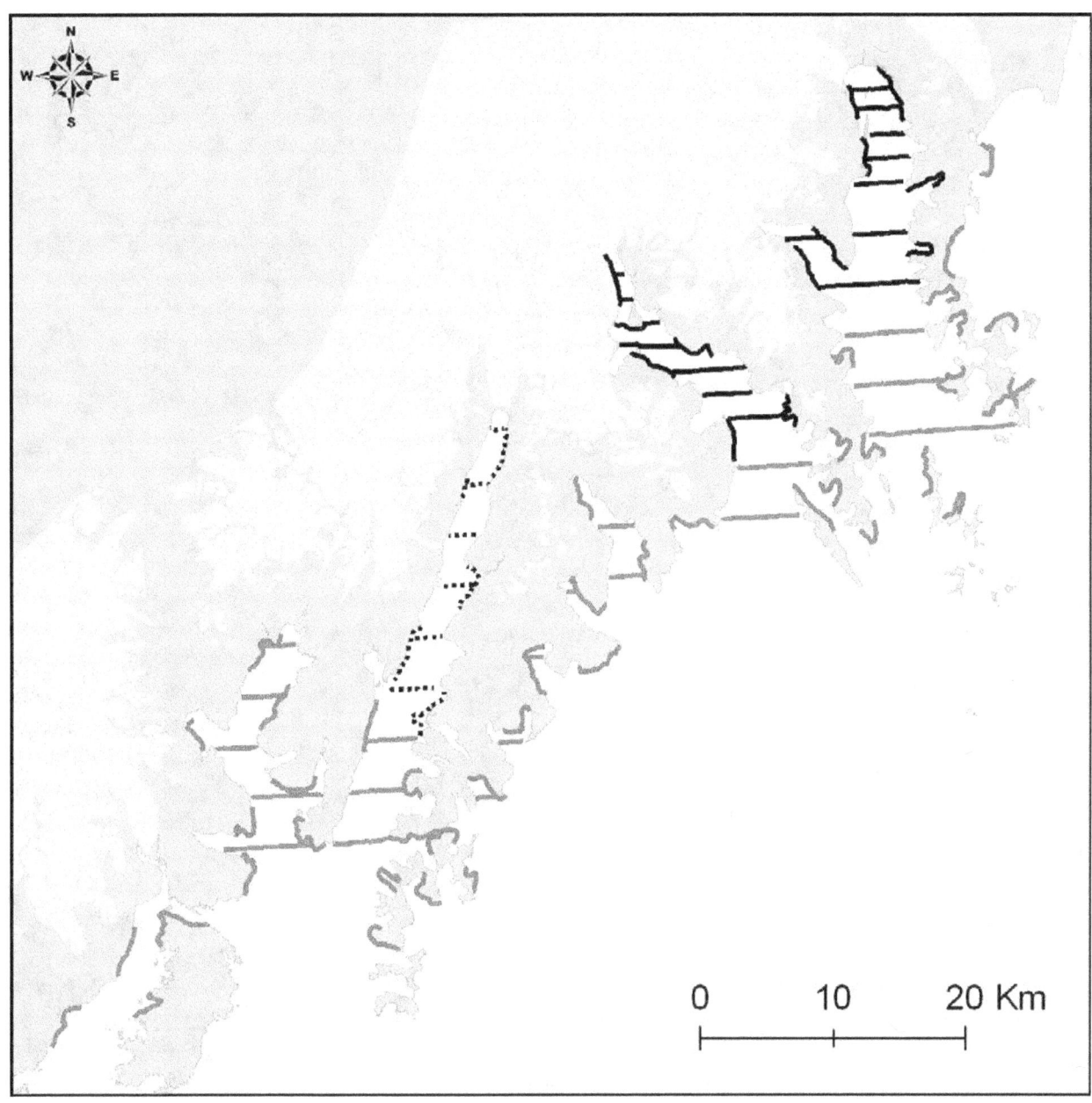

Figure 2. Map showing marine bird transect locations in Kenai Fjords National Park, Alaska, summers 2006–08. Population estimates for Kittlitz's and marbled murrelets were derived from mid-season surveys (red, black, and dashed lines). A subset of transects (black lines) was surveyed in the early and late/fledgling seasons each year, and transects in the East Arm of Nuka Bay (dashed lines) were not surveyed during all sampling periods because of poor weather.

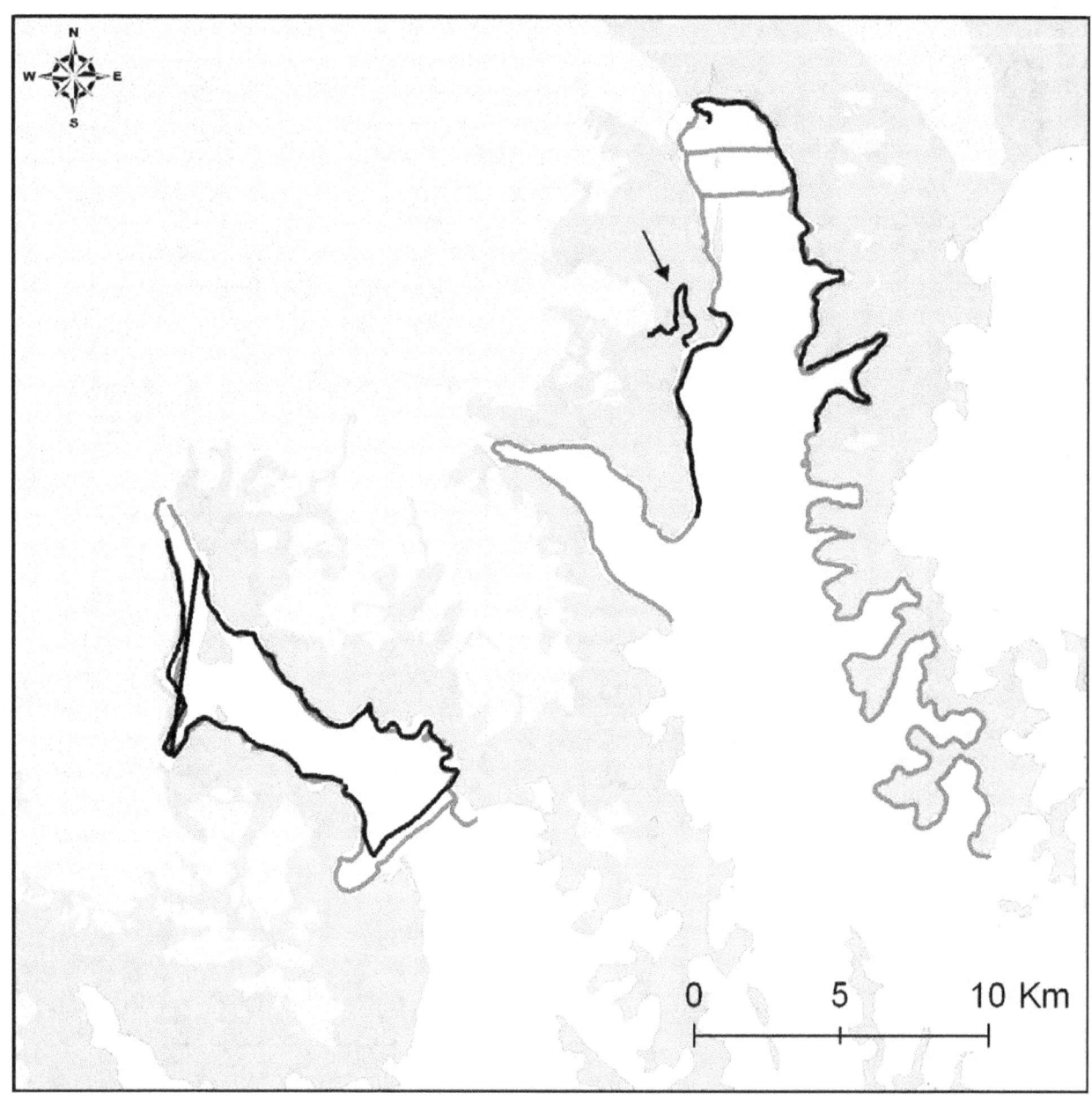

Figure 3. Map showing fledgling survey lines in Aialik Bay and Northwestern Lagoon, Alaska, 2007. Blue stipple represents ice extent and a black arrow indicates a survey within Pederson Lagoon.

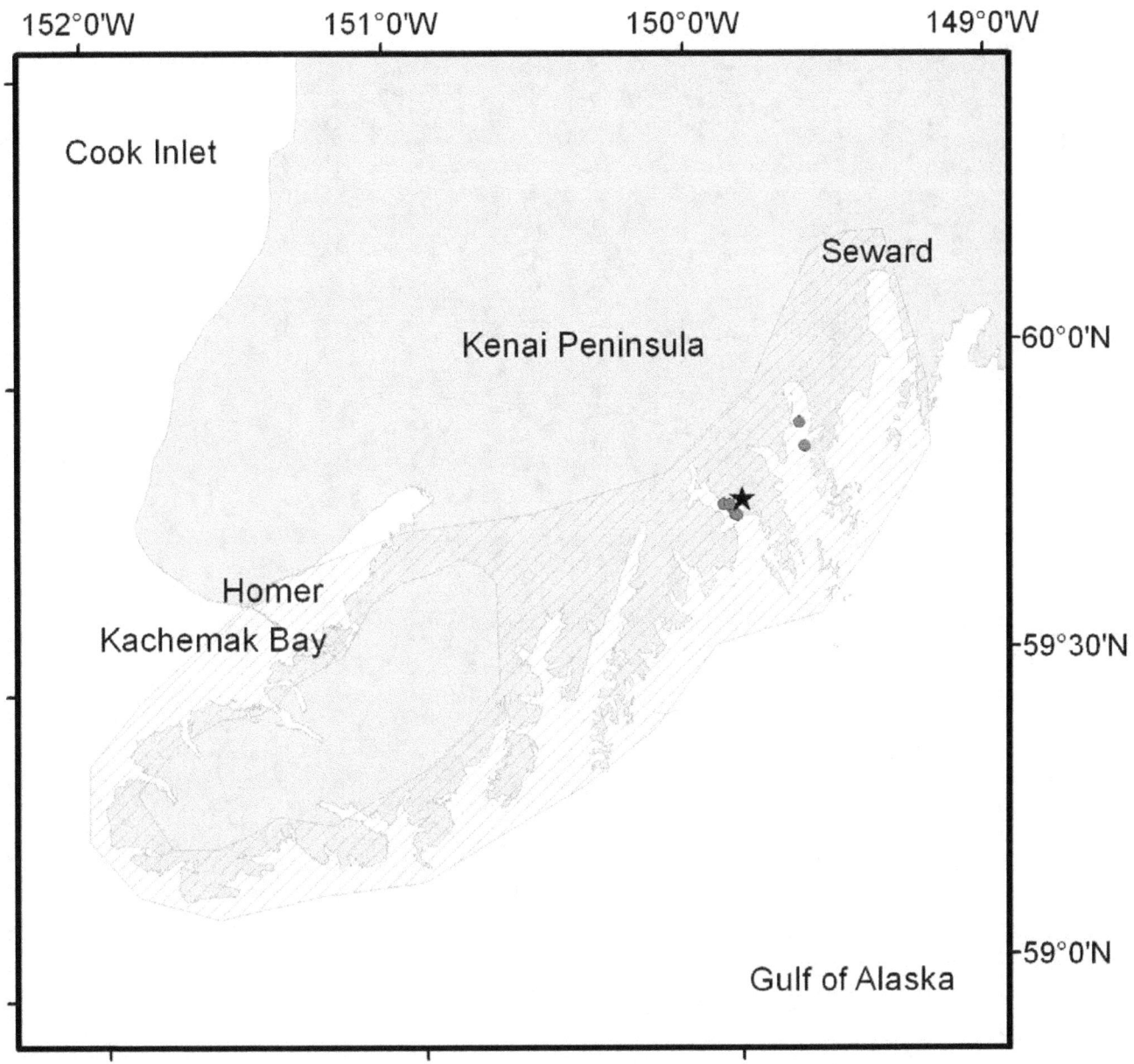

Figure 4. Map showing approximate area (blue) covered by boat-based and aerial relocation surveys for radio-marked Kittlitz's murrelets in the lower Kenai Peninsula area, May 10–July 1, 2006. Red circles indicate capture locations, and a black star indicates a possible nest site.

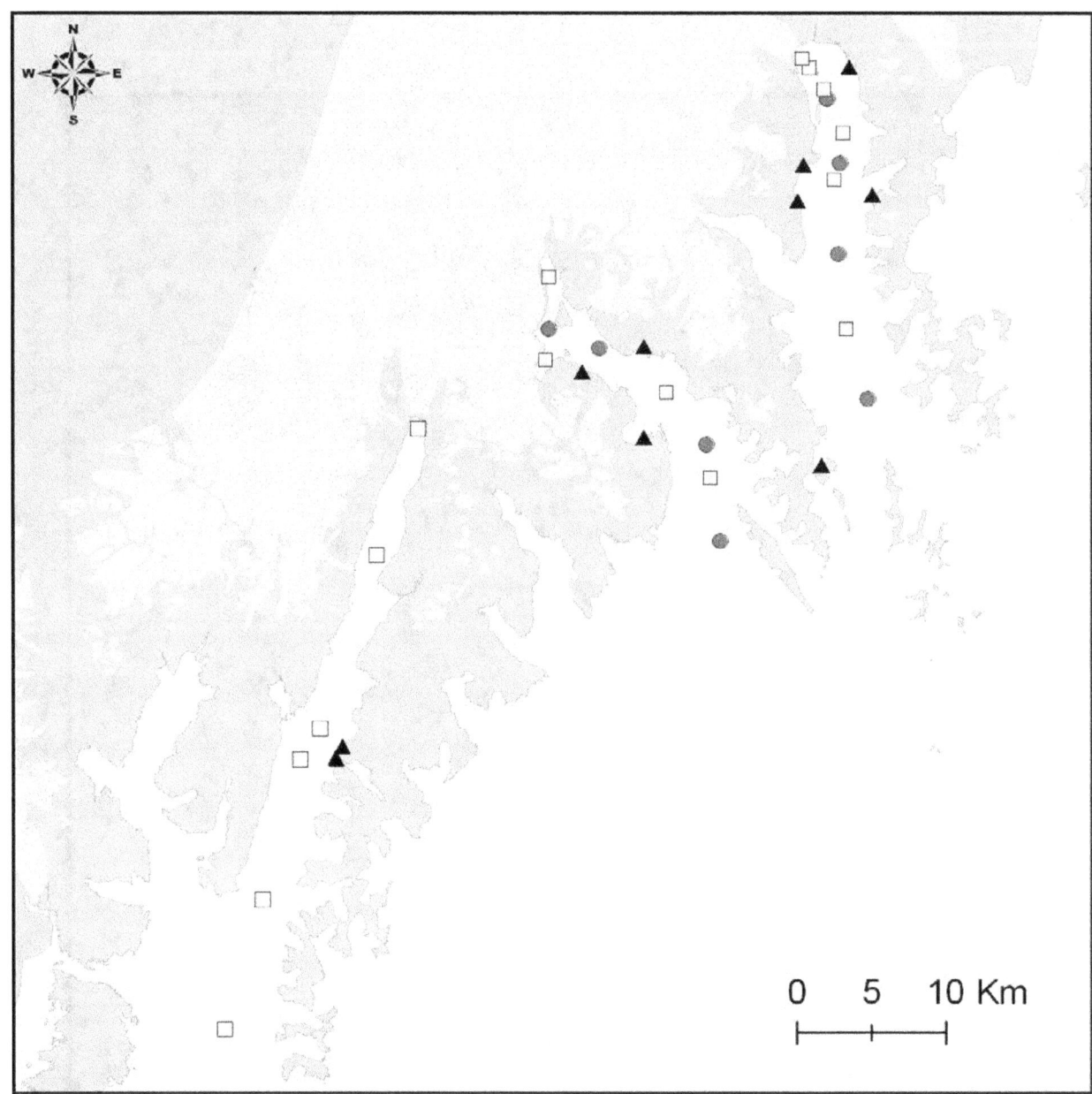

Figure 5. Map showing beach seine (triangles), oceanography stations (squares), and large Isaacs-Kidd Midwater Trawl (IKMT, red circles) stations sampled in Kenai Fjords, Alaska. Open squares indicate conductivity-temperature-depth (CTD) stations in the East Arm of Nuka Bay that were sampled in 2007 only, and yellow squares were sampled in 2007 and 2008. CTD casts and water samples also were collected at IKMT stations.

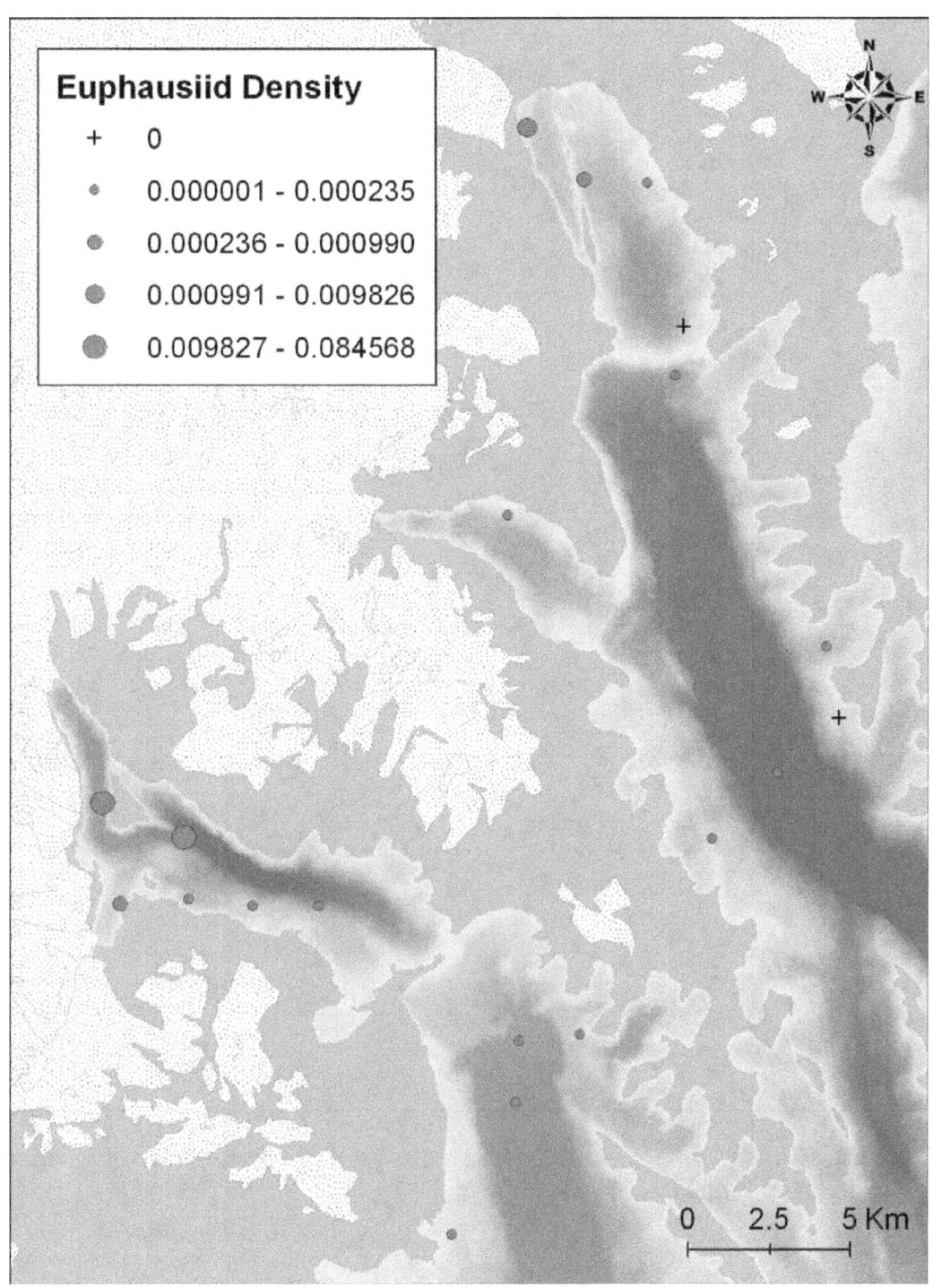

Figure 6. Map showing large Isaacs-Kidd midwater trawl locations (red circles and black crosses), and euphausiid density (#/m³) during sampling, Kenai Fjords, Alaska, June 29–July 3, 2007. Bathymetric features are indicated in blue, with darker shades denoting deeper bottom depth. Ice extent is indicated by blue stipple.

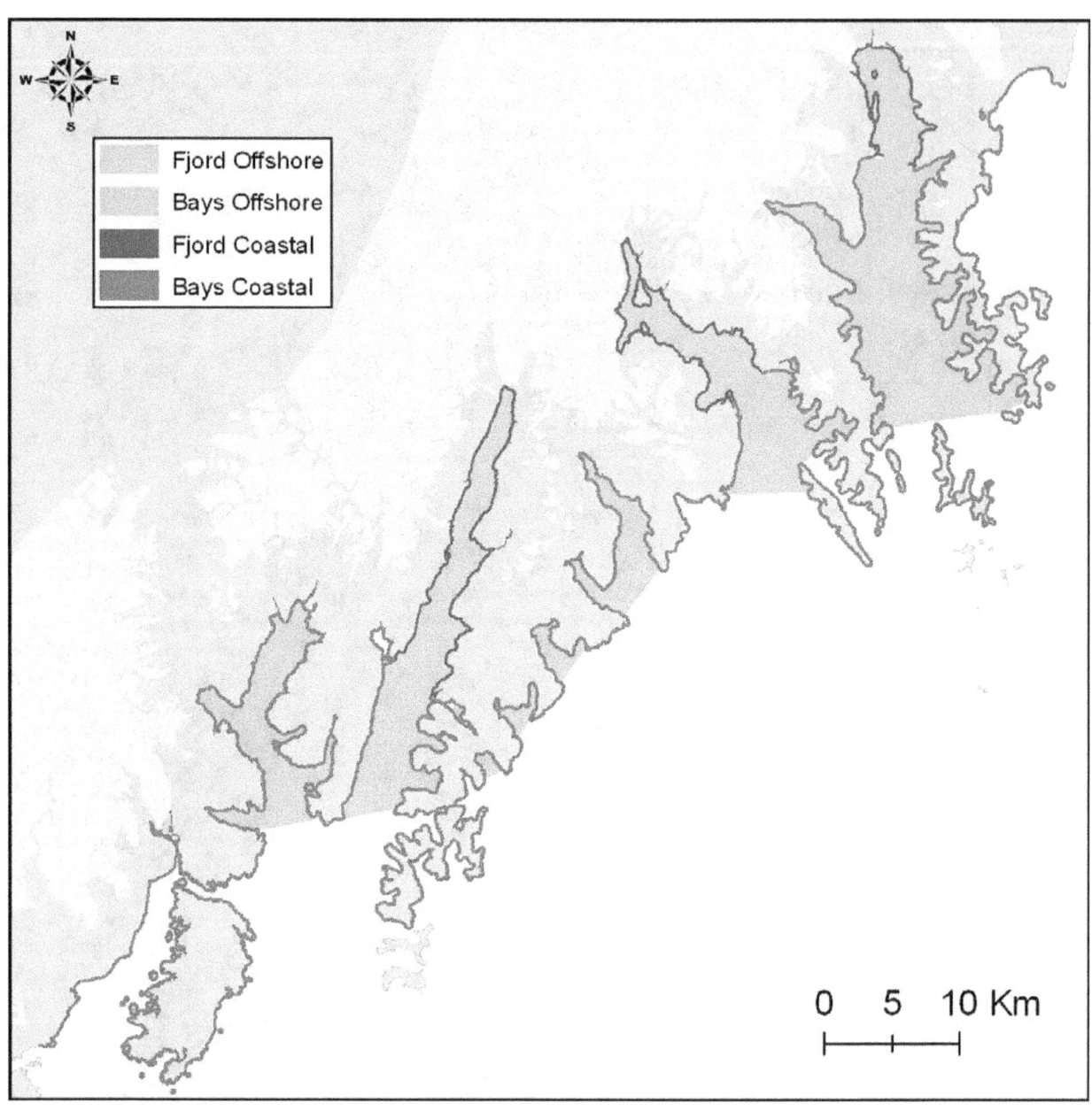

Figure 7. Map showing strata used to generate population estimates for Kittlitz's and marbled murrelets, Kenai Fjords National Park, Alaska, 2006–08.

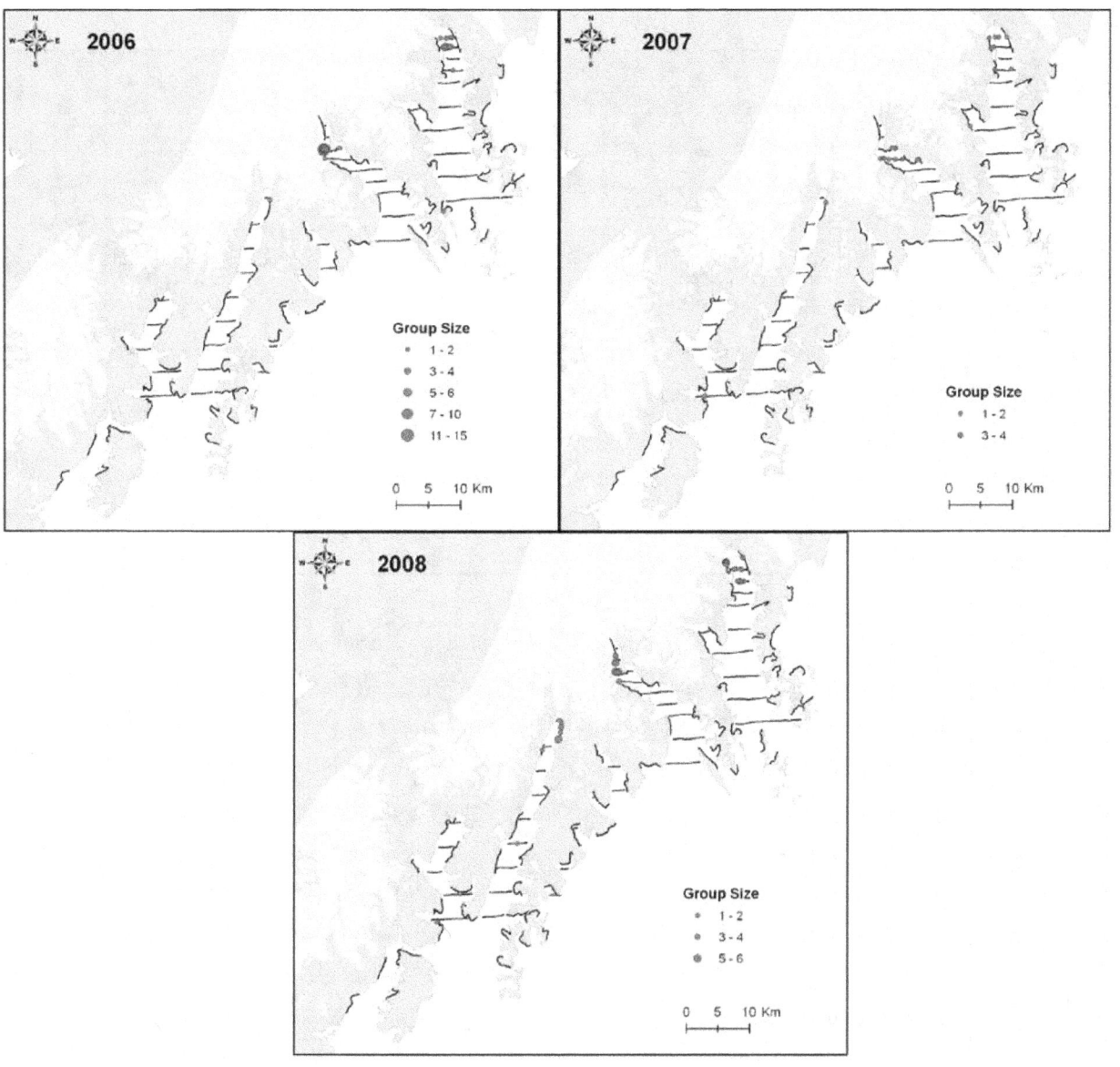

Figure 8. Maps showing Kittlitz's murrelet distribution during mid-season coastwide surveys, Kenai Fjords, Alaska. Transect lines are indicated by black lines and glacial extent is in blue stipple.

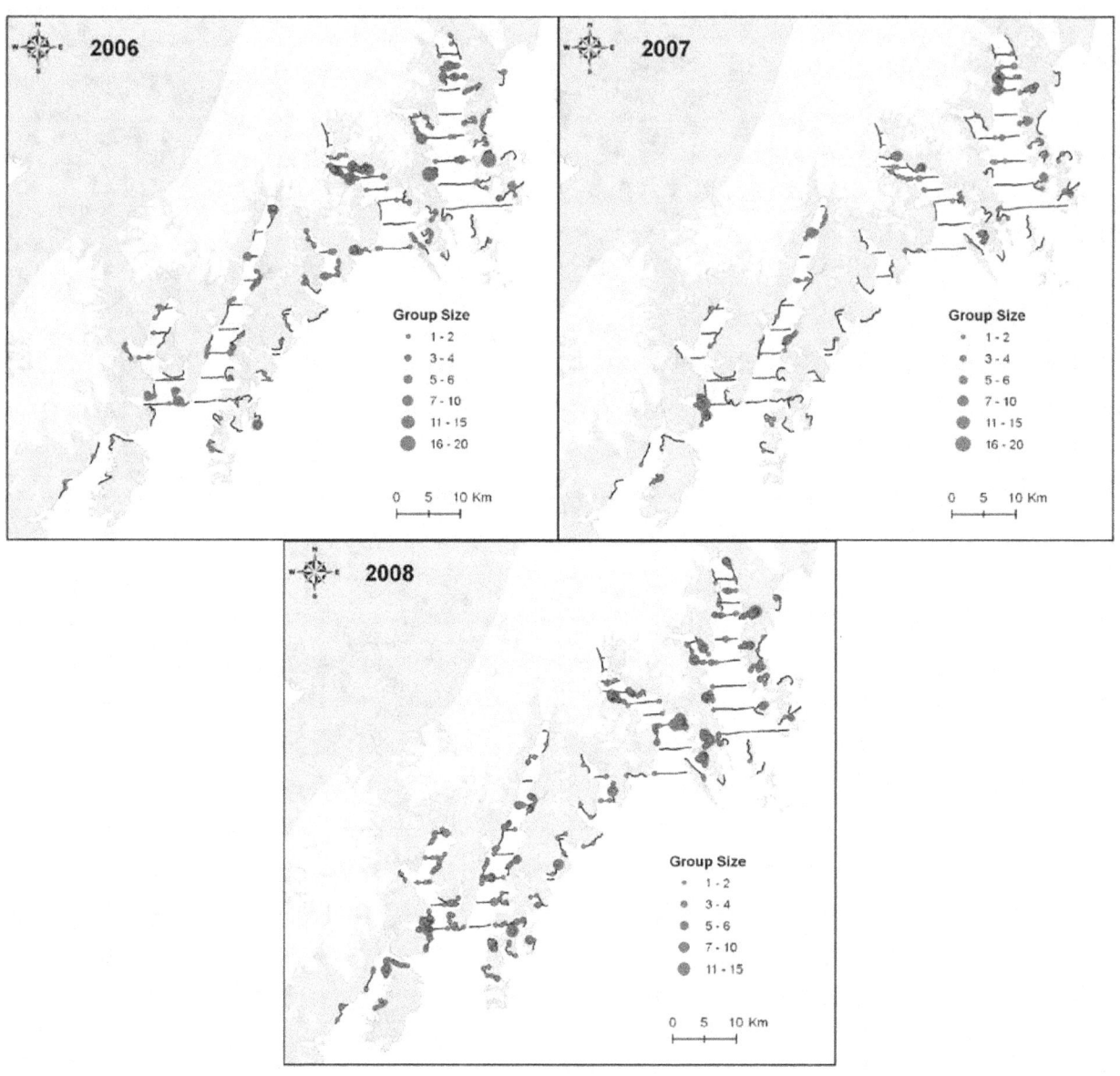

Figure 9. Maps showing Marbled murrelet distribution during mid-season coastwide surveys, Kenai Fjords, Alaska. Transects are indicated by black lines, and glacial extent is in blue stipple.

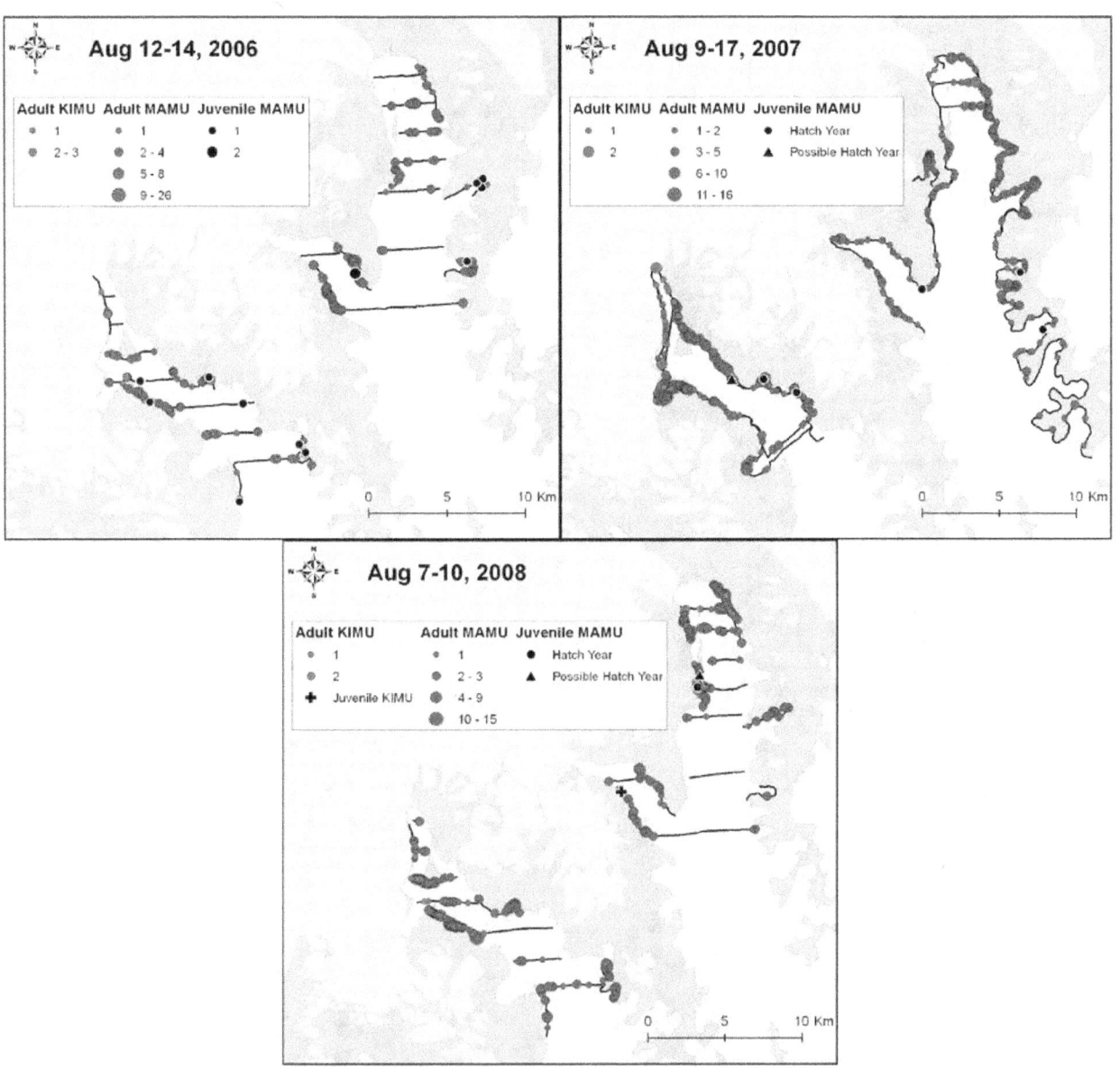

Figure 10. Maps showing Kittlitz's murrelet (KIMU) and marbled murrelet (MAMU) distribution, including adult and juvenile records, during fledging period surveys in Northwestern Fjord and Aialik Bay, Kenai Fjords, Alaska.

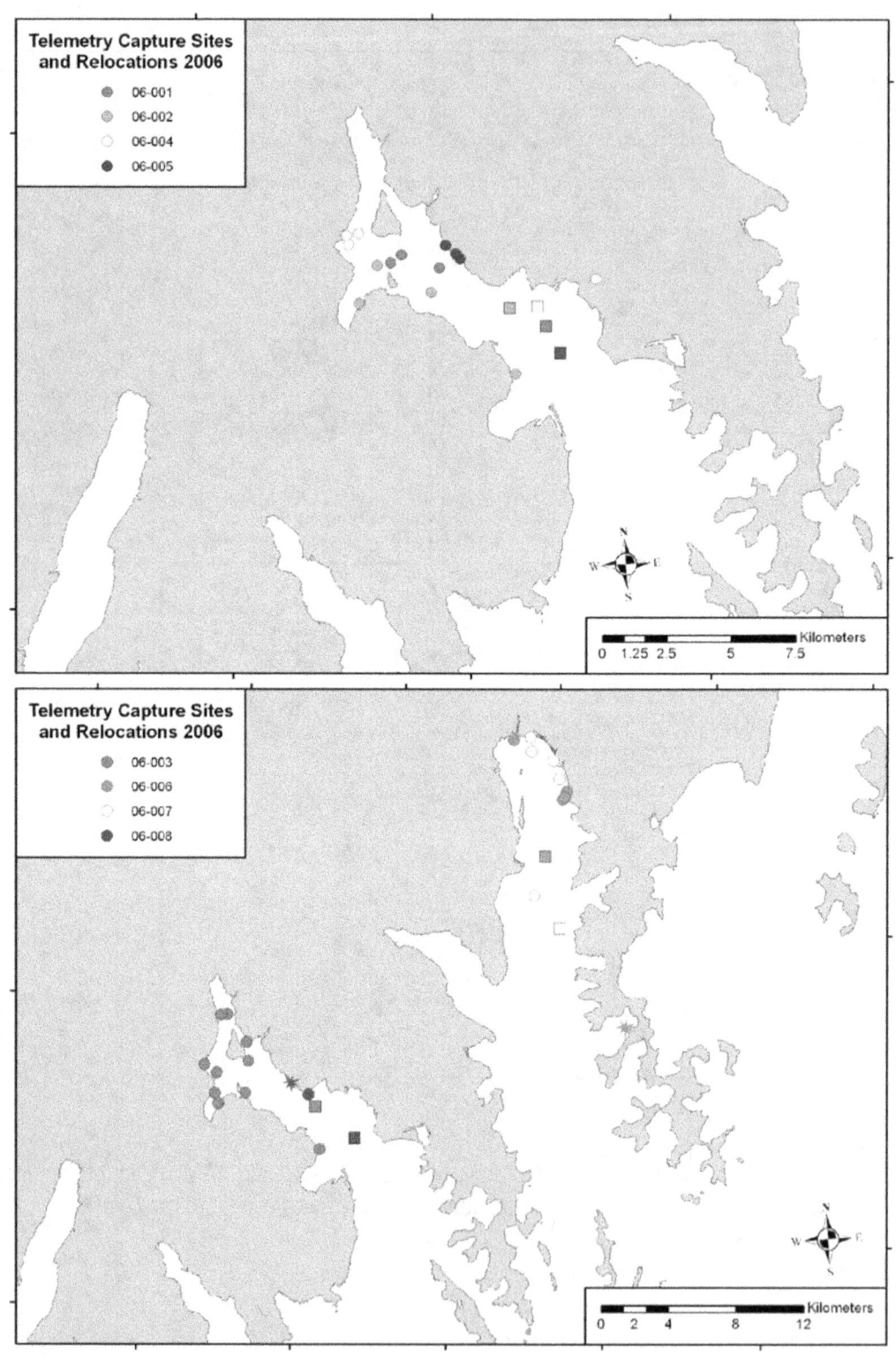

Figure 11. Maps showing location of radio-marked Kittlitz's murrelets (circles) tracked by boat-based and aerial telemetry searches, and capture locations (squares), Kenai Fjords, Alaska, 2006. Top and bottom panels represent different birds. Star symbols indicate mortalities.

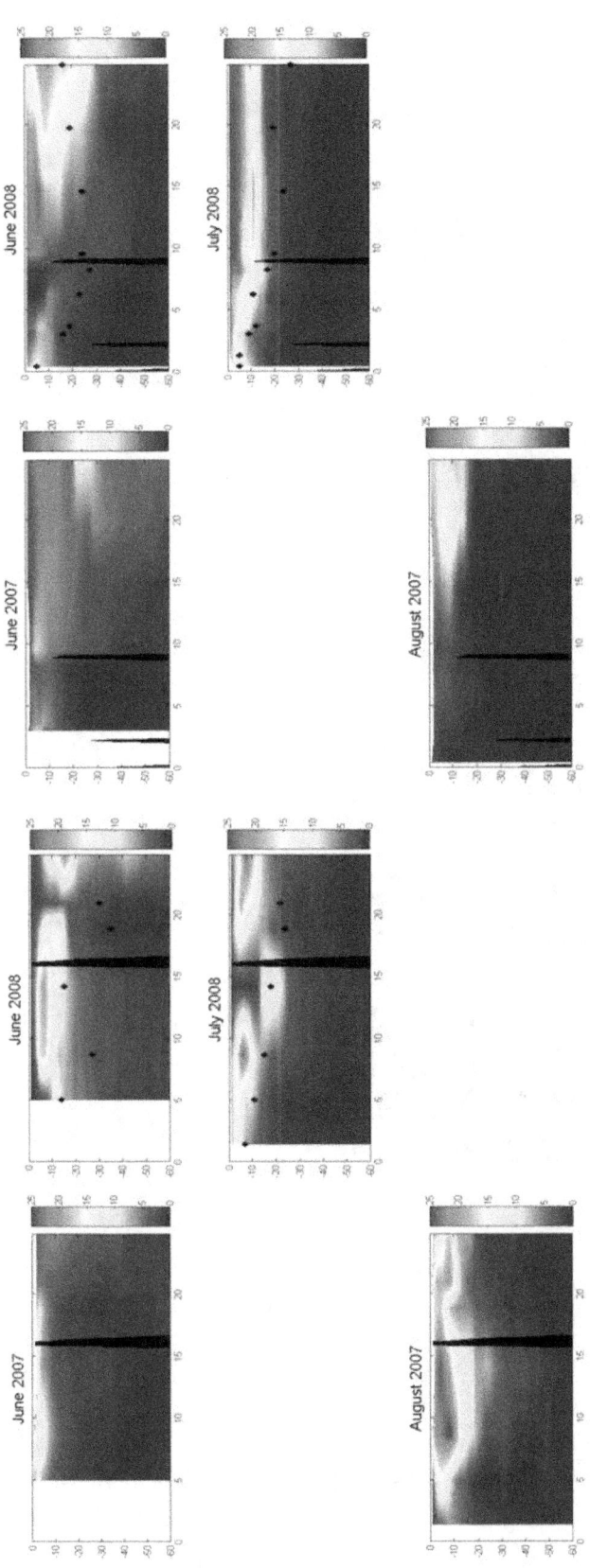

Figure 12. Graphs showing temperature (color) and salinity (line) vertical contours relative to bottom depth (m, x-axis) and glacier distance (y-axis) in Northwestern Fjord (two left panels) and Aialik Bay (two right panels), Alaska. Bathymetric features are indicated in solid black.

41

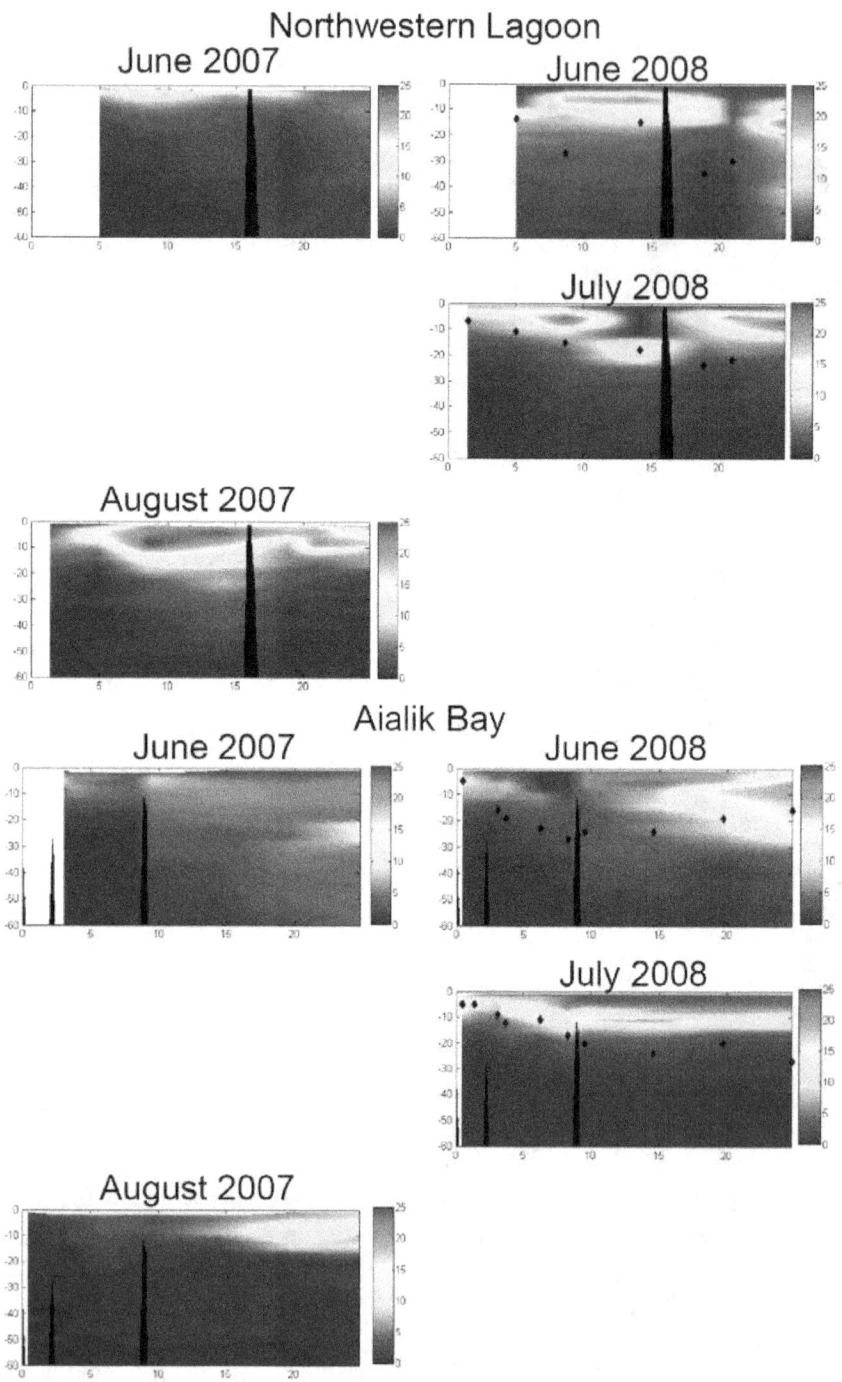

Figure 13. Chlorophyll a vertical contours relative to depth (m, y-axis), and distance to tidewater glacier (km, x-axis) in Kenai Fjords National Park, Alaska. Photic depth is indicated as black diamonds, and position of the sill is indicated in solid black.

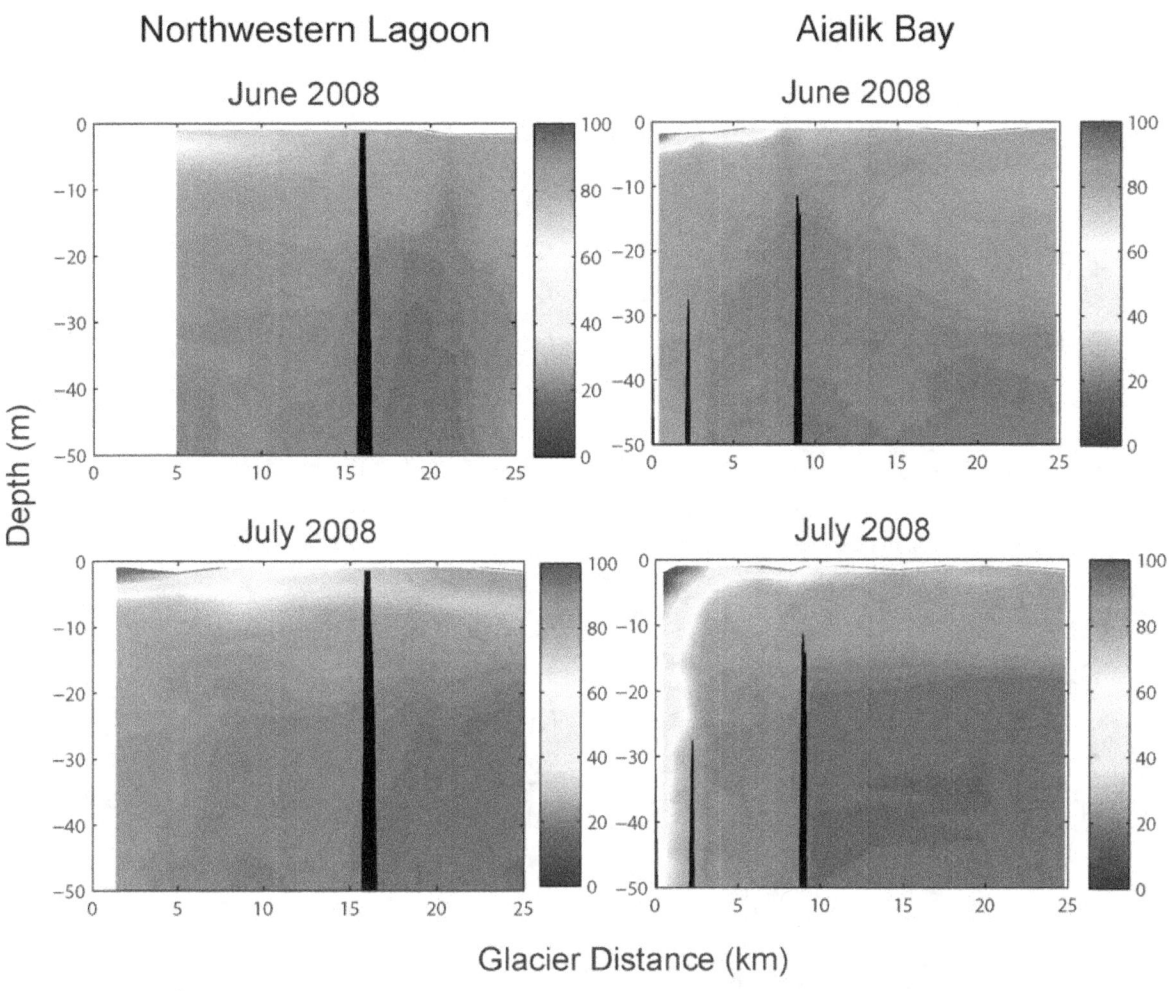

Figure 14. Water clarity vertical contours (beam transmission, %) relative to depth (m, y-axis) and distance to tidewater glaciers (km, x-axis), Kenai Fjords National Park, Alaska. Bathymetric features are indicated in black.

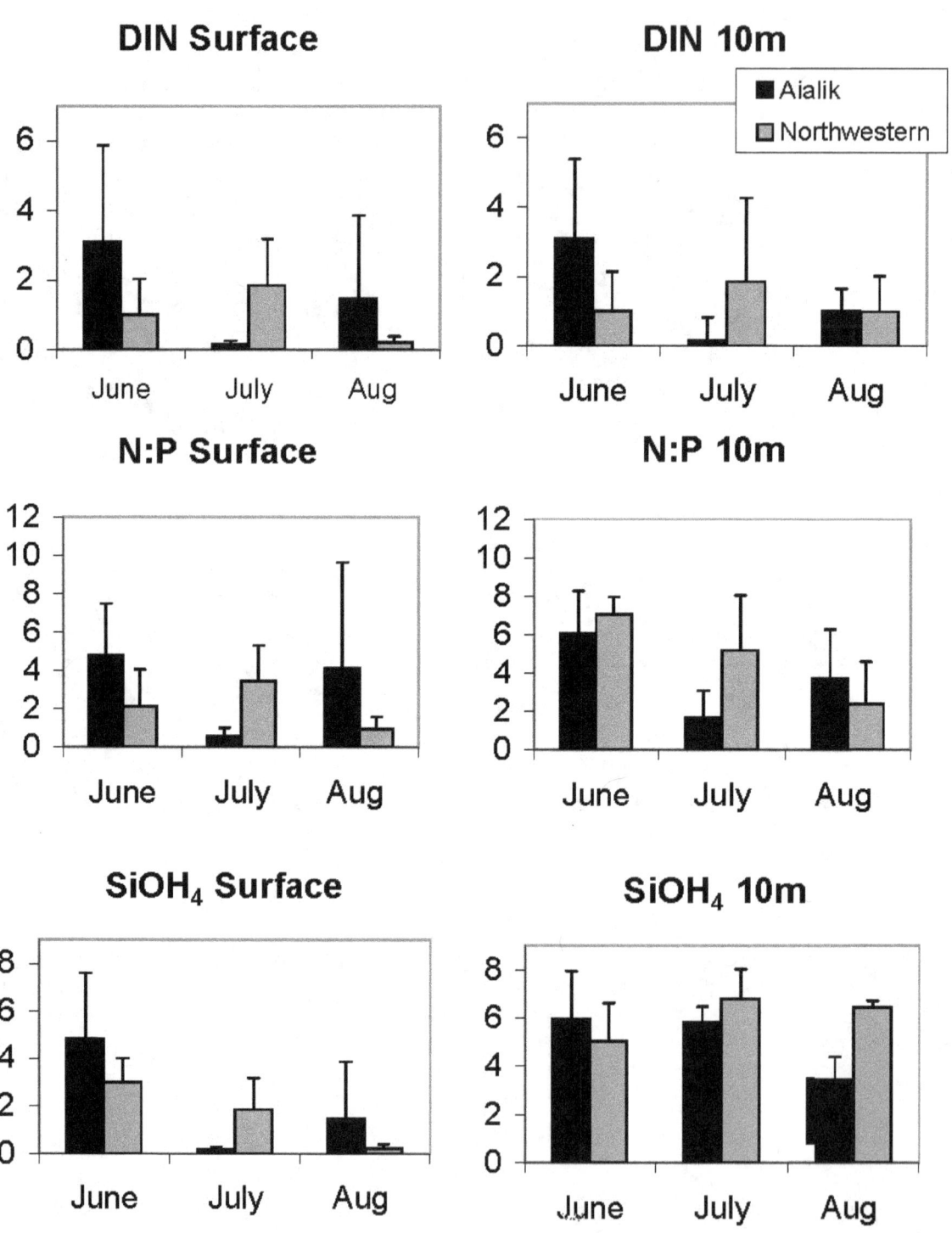

Figure 15. Graphs showing monthly average (SD) dissolved inorganic nitrogen (DIN, µM), nitrogen to phosphate ratio (N:P), and silicic acid (SiOH₄, µM) values in Aialik Bay and Northwestern Fjord, Alaska, 2008.

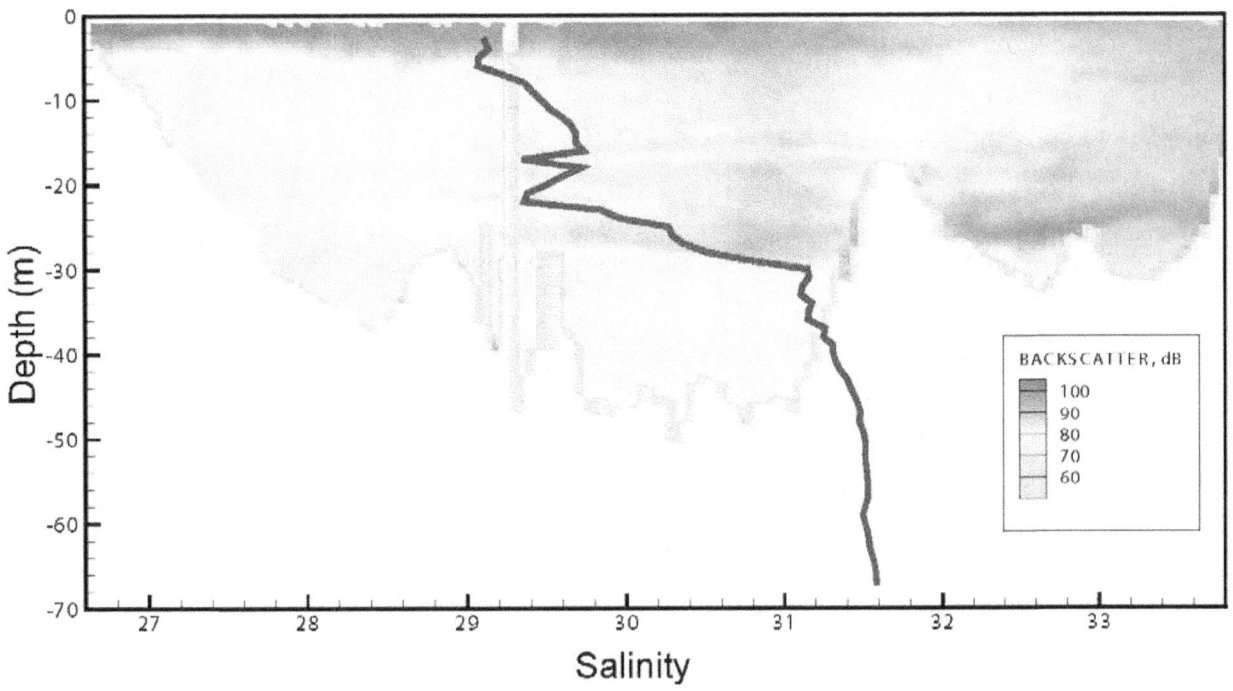

Figure 16. Graph showing backscatter vertical profile (color, decibels, dB) measured by an acoustic Doppler current profiler and salinity data measured at the front of Aialik Glacier, Alaska, August 14, 2007. The left side of the graph represents the south side of the fjord.

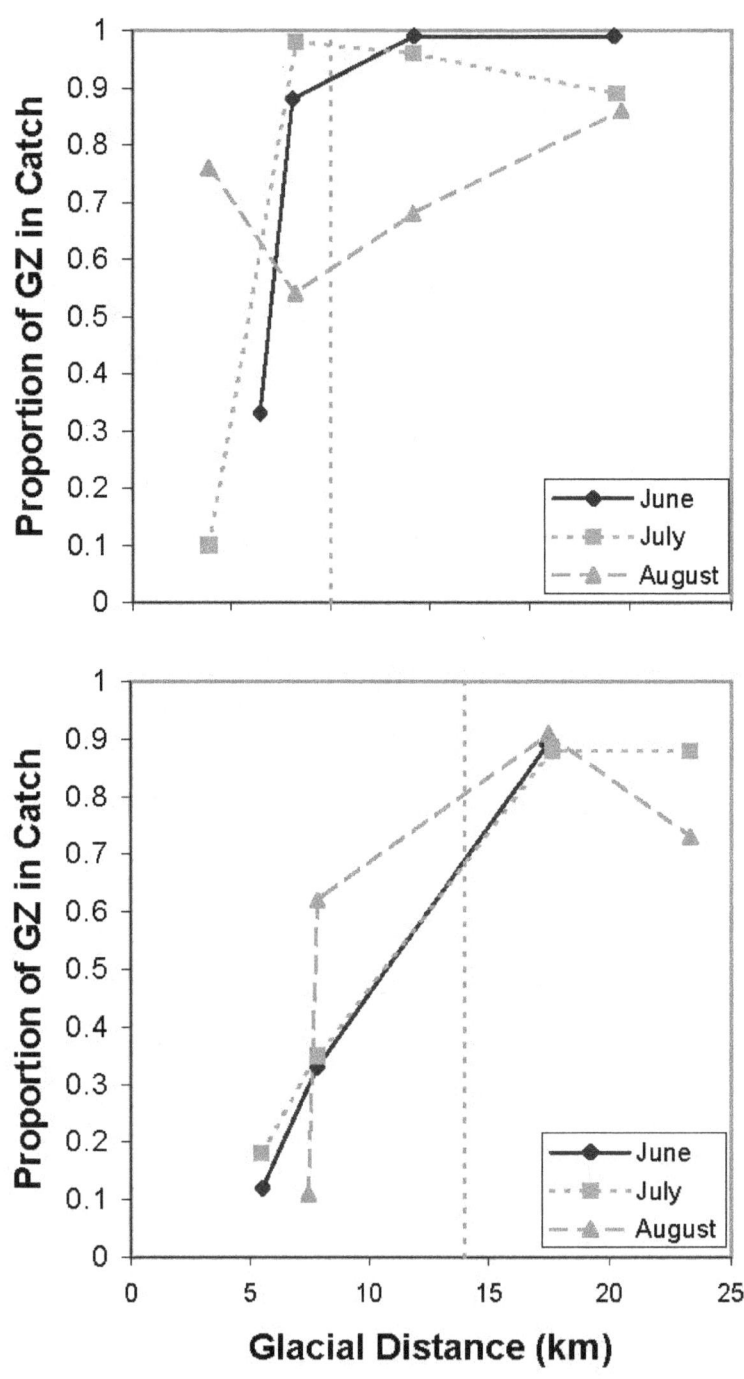

Figure 17. Graphs showing proportion of Isaacs-Kidd midwater trawl catches that were comprised of gelatinous zooplankton (GZ) relative to distance to nearest tidewater glacier in Aialik Bay (upper) and Northwestern Lagoon (lower), Alaska, 2008. The approximate location of the marine sills are indicated as a vertical grey dotted line.

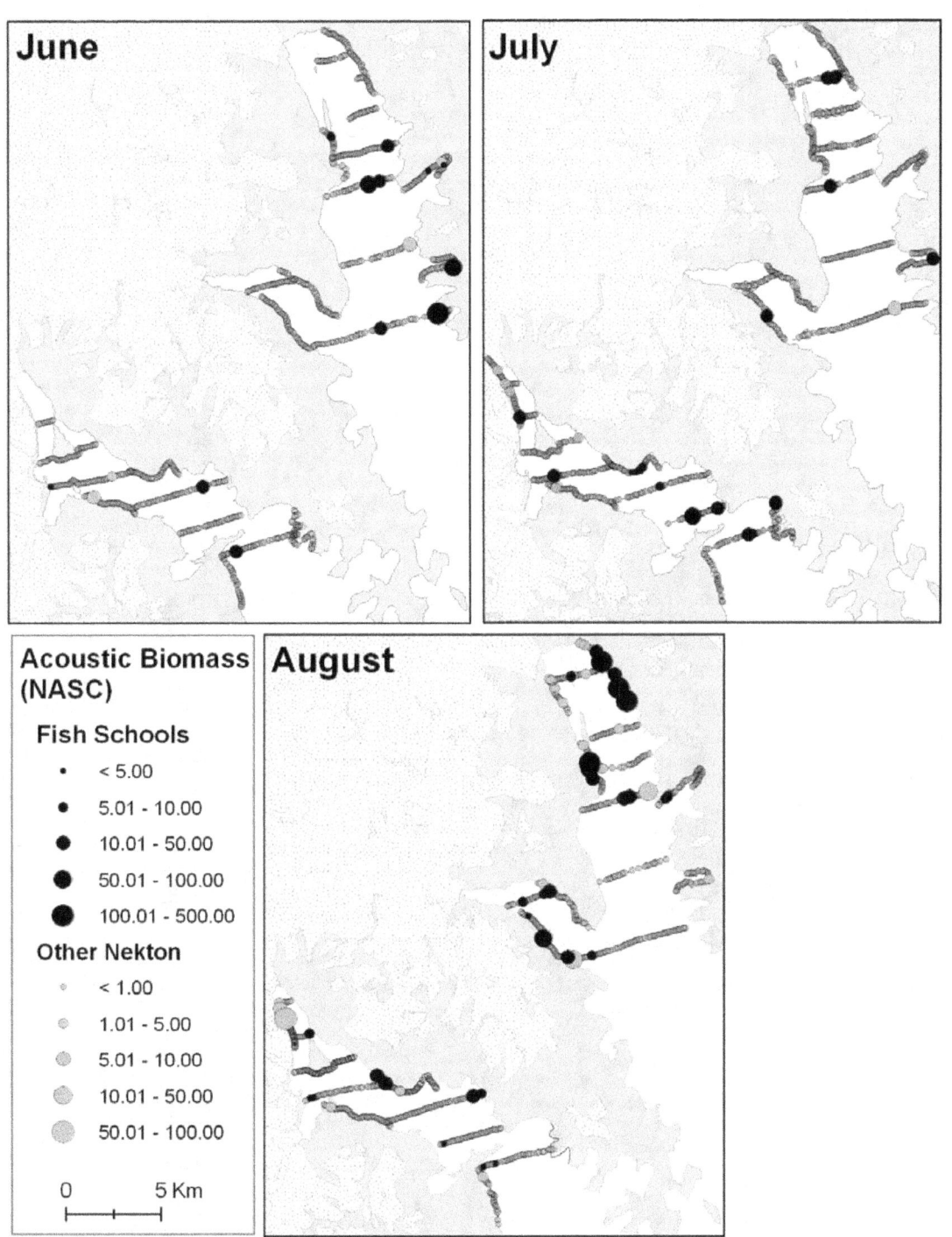

Figure 18. Maps showing monthly hydroacoustic backscatter (nautical area scattering coefficient, NASC) due to dense forage schools and weaker scattering nekton measured in Kenai Fjords, Alaska, 2008.

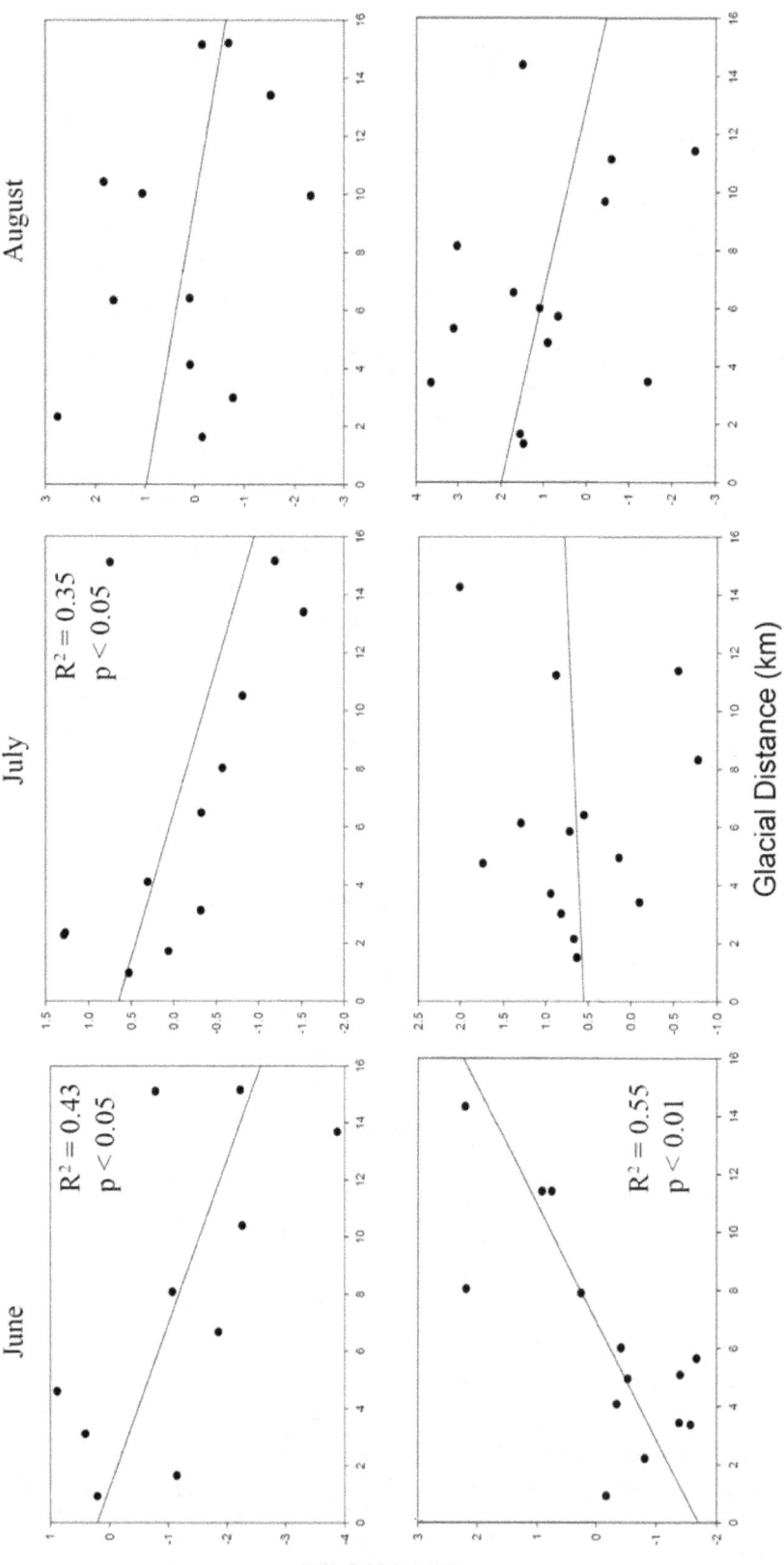

Figure 19. Graphs showing monthly relationship between acoustic backscatter and transect distance to tidewater glaciers in Northwestern Lagoon (top panel) and Aialik Bay (bottom panel), Kenai Fjords National Park, Alaska, 2008.

48

Table 1. Summary of at-sea survey effort in Kenai Fjords National Park, Alaska, during summers of 2006–08.

[km^2, square kilometer; km, kilometer]

Year	Survey	Survey dates	Number of transects	Survey area (km^2)	Survey length (km)
2006	Early Season Coastwide (mid-season)	5/31–6/2	36	25.64	128.2
		6/27–7/5	100	78.54	392.7
	Late Season	7/31–8/1 and 8/13	25	18.74	93.7
	Fledgling	8/12 and 8/14	13	9.9	49.5
2007	Early Season Coastwide (mid-season)	6/1–6/8	33	23.38	116.9
		6/25–6/29	90	72.94	364.7
	Late Season	7/31–8/4	37	24.58	122.9
	Fledgling	8/9–8/17	21	51.3	256.5
2008	Early Season Coastwide (mid-season)	6/4–6/8	25	17.54	87.7
		7/5–7/15	99	74.44	372.2
	Late Season	8/7–8/10	27	19	95.0

Table 2. Summary of mid-season, coastwide surveys conducted in Kenai Fjords National Park, Alaska, during summers of 2006–08.

[km^2, square kilometer; km, kilometer; %, percent]

Stratum	Distance surveyed (km)	Number of transects	Area surveyed (km^2)	Area of stratum (km^2)	Proportion sampled (%)
Fjords Coastal	45.6	12	9.1	29.6	30.8
Coastline	191.4	45	38.3	161.3	23.7
Fjords Offshore	42.1	15	8.4	103.0	8.2
Bays Offshore	113.7	28	22.7	320.6	7.1
2006 Total	392.8	100	78.6	614.5	12.8
Fjords Coastal	39.5	11	7.9	29.6	26.7
Coastline	186.2	40	37.24	161.3	23.1
Fjords Offshore	43.4	17	8.68	103	8.4
Bays Offshore	95.6	22	19.12	320.6	6.0
2007 Total	364.7	90	72.94	614.5	11.9
Fjords Coastal	42.5	11	8.5	29.6	28.7
Coastline	203.9	49	40.78	161.3	25.3
Fjords Offshore	36.8	15	7.36	103	7.1
Bays Offshore	88.9	24	17.78	320.6	5.5
2008 Total	372.1	99	74.4	614.5	12.1

Table 3. Population estimates (95%-confidence intervals) and coefficients of variation (%) for *Brachyramphus murrelets* in Kenai Fjords National Park, Alaska, 2006–08.

[Species abbreviations are Kittlitz's murrelet (KIMU), marbled murrelet (MAMU), and all *Brachyramphus* murrelets combined (BRMU). Total estimates are based on the sum of line transect estimates for birds sighted on the water and strip transect estimates for birds sighted in the air. Detection probabilities for line transect estimates were modeled using observations of all BRMU sighted within 100 meters of the survey vessel]

Year	Behavior	KIMU		MAMU		BRMU	
		N (95% CI)	CV	N (95% CI)	CV	N (95% CI)	CV
2006	Water	740 (268–2,042)	55.7	6,082 (4,416–8,376)	16.4	6,930 (4,737–10,136)	19.6
	Fly	185 (63–539)	67.6	336 (184–614)	31.5	656 (409–1,052)	24.4
	Adjusted Estimate	925 (393–2,179)	45.9	6,418 (4,730–8,709)	15.6	7,586 (5,344–10,768)	18.0
2007	Water	407 (239–694)	27.8	3,460 (2,228–5,373)	22.7	4,224 (2,915–6,121)	19.1
	Fly	16 (4–61)	77.4	159 (59–367)	44.7	200 (99–402)	36.8
	Adjusted Estimate	423 (252–709)	26.8	3,619 (2,371–5,524)	21.8	4,424 (3,099–6,315)	18.3
2008	Water	664 (294–1,499)	43.4	7,441 (5,463–10,136)	15.9	9,290 (7,086–12,180)	13.9
	Fly		0	88 (32–240)	54.7	387 (196–763)	35.7
	Adjusted Estimate	664 (294–1,499)	43.4	7,529 (5,546–10,222)	15.7	9,677 (7,449–12,571)	13.4

Table 4. Proportion (percent) of *Brachyramphus murrelets* (all behaviors, and flying birds only) that were Kittlitz's murrelets (KIMU), marbled murrelets (MAMU), and unidentified *Brachyramphus* Murrelets (UNMU) observed within 100 meters of the vessel during Kenai Fjords surveys, Alaska, 2006–08.

Year	Survey period	Observations of all murrelets			Observations of flying murrelets		
		KIMU	MAMU	UNMU	KIMU	MAMU	UNMU
2006	Early	23.4	74.9	1.8	4.2	2.1	60.0
	Middle	14.6	83.8	1.6	19.8	4.7	60.0
	Late	3.6	93.7	2.7	0.0	0.9	82.4
2007	Early	10.7	85.7	3.6	0.0	1.8	37.5
	Middle	11.7	78.9	9.4	5.4	2.8	10.8
	Late	3.5	93.0	3.5	2.6	3.9	18.3
2008	Early	13.5	82.8	3.7	2.4	2.0	35.7
	Middle	14.3	79.5	6.2	0.0	0.6	14.0
	Late	2.6	93.3	4.0	0.0	0.7	25.0

Table 5. Within season density estimates (D, birds/km²), confidence intervals (CI), and coefficients of variation (CV, %) for Kittlitz's murrelets (KIMU), marbled murrelets (MAMU) in Kenai Fjords National Park, Alaska, 2006–08.

[Estimates were derived from the raw counts and counts that were prorated for unidentified birds by transect. km², square kilometer]

Year	Survey period	KIMU D (95% CI)	CV	MAMU D (95% CI)	CV
2006	Early	2.34 (0.99–4.04)	34.2	12.16 (8.14 – 16.48)	18.1
	Middle	3.67 (0.28–9.19)	64.8	16.12 (8.28–26.87)	29.6
	Late	0.74 (0.17–1.45)	44.2	24.09 (15.44–33.87)	20.3
2007	Early	3.26 (1.08–5.91)	39.9	19.11 (12.72–26.70)	19.2
	Middle	1.40 (0.32–2.97)	49.0	12.63 (6.90–19.66)	24.8
	Late	1.81 (0.82–3.29)	34.4	47.88 (34.44–65.12)	16.3
2008	Early	2.61 (1.04–4.40)	32.6	9.98 (5.31–15.61)	26.1
	Middle	2.94 (0.99–5.95)	42.4	18.40 (12.54–25.30)	18.0
	Late	0.76 (0.15–1.69)	54.6	29.68 (18.60–45.13)	21.9
		Prorated KIMU		**Prorated MAMU**	
2006	Early	2.44 (1.08–4.43)	34.4	12.26 (8.59–17.11)	18.5
	Middle	3.67 (0.23–9.66)	67.7	16.16 (8.54–26.34)	28.8
	Late	0.74 (0.18–1.52)	44.6	24.31 (16.12–36.11)	20.7
2007	Early	3.56 (1.13–6.53)	38.4	20.41 (13.76–29.61)	20.1
	Middle	1.55 (0.43–3.23)	46.9	12.77 (7.57–19.34)	23.6
	Late	2.05 (0.91–3.66)	35.3	50.81 (35.49–68.34)	16.6
2008	Early	2.73 (1.12–4.66)	33.2	10.33 (5.81–15.53)	24.7
	Middle	3.33 (1.08–6.14)	40.0	20.45 (13.84–28.06)	18.5
	Late	0.76 (0.17–1.81)	53.5	30.80 (19.93–45.73)	20.9

Table 6. Average density (SE) within strata across years for Kittlitz's murrelets (KIMU), marbled murrelets (MAMU), and all *Brachyramphus* murrelets combined (BRMU) during mid-season coastwide surveys in Kenai Fjords, Alaska, 2006–08.

Stratum	KIMU	MAMU	BRMU
Bays coastal	0.02 (0.01)	13.19 (4.36)	14.49 (5.30)
Bays Offshore	0.02 (0.02)	6.39 (1.60)	7.15 (1.85)
Fjord Offshore	5.97 (1.58)	9.16 (3.12)	16.73 (3.74)
Fjord Coastal	1.61 (1.05)	25.32 (4.00)	30.15 (3.28)

Table 7. Kittlitz's murrelet measurements from May 2006 in Kenai Fjords compared to May 2004 in Glacier Bay, Alaska.

[g, gram; mm, millimeter; asterisk*, $p < 0.05$]

Data source		Body mass (g)	Tarsus (mm)	Wing chord (mm)	Culmen (mm)
2006 Kenai Fjords	Mean	222.3	18.2	140.9	10.7
N=8	Std Err	6.2*	0.2	1.2	0.2
2004 Glacier Bay	Mean	238.9	17.6	139.4	11.1
N=20	Std Err	4.3*	0.2	1	0.3

Table 8. Nutrient concentrations (µM) sampled in Northwestern Lagoon and Aialik Bay, Alaska, 2008.

[SE, standard error; m, meters; µM, micro moles per liter]

Nutrient	Range	Surface Mean	SE	Range	10 m Mean	SE
Phosphate	0.140–0.870	0.368	0.035	0.210–0.900	0.519	0.044
Silicic Acid	1.980–9.270	4.439	0.362	2.620–8.420	5.557	0.34
Nitrate	0–5.190	0.512	0.215	0.070–4.800	1.446	0.329
Nitrite	0–0.120	0.03	0.006	0–0.150	0.054	0.011
Ammonium	0.010–4.920	0.776	0.224	0.010–3.510	1.131	0.209

Table 9. Species, size (fork length, mm), and sample size (n) of fishes captured in small and large Isaacs-Kidd midwater trawls (IKMT), Kenai Fjords, Alaska, 2007–08.

[SD, standard deviation; n, sample size]

Common Name	Scientific Name	Small IKMT		Large IKMT	
		Size Range (n)	Average (SD)	Size Range (n)	Average (SD)
Pacific herring	*Clupea pallasii*	–	–	14–22 (5)	17 (3.1)
Northern smoothtongue	*Leuroglossus schmidti*	27 (1)	27	–	–
Capelin	*Mallotus villosus*	–	–	5–30 (845)	14 (5.3)
Eulachon	*Thaleichthys pacificus*	26 (1)	26	–	–
Larval smelt	*Osmeridae (Family)*	26 (1)	26	14 (1)	14
Lanternfish	*Myctophidae (Family)*	–	–	15 (1)	15
Saffron cod	*Eleginus gracilis*	12–51 (97)	31 (9.8)	7–69 (55)	24 (19.1)
Walleye pollock	*Theragra chalcogramma*	17–41 (86)	25 (4.5)	7–16 (24)	10 (2.7)
Pacific cod	*Gadus macrocephalus*	33–36 (2)	35 (2.1)	12 (1)	12
Gadid	*Gadidae (Family)*	12–32 (32)	22 (5.2)	–	–
Rockfish	*Sebastes spp.*	11–19 (6)	14 (3.2)	–	–
Spinyhead sculpin	*Dasycottus setiger*	12–25 (142)	14 (3.2)	25–30 (31)	28 (1.4)
Padded sculpin	*Artedius fenestralis*	–	–	14 (1)	14
Sculpin	*Cottidae (family)*	–	–	7–12 (4)	10 (2.2)
Soft sculpin	*Psychrolutes sigalutes*	12–54 (4)	34 (19.0)	35–48 (2)	42 (9.2)
Crested sculpin	*Blepsias bilobus*	21–27 (5)	24 (2.2)	–	–
Silverspotted sculpin	*Blepsias cirrhosus*	–	–	13 (1)	13
Northern ronquil	*Ronquilus jordani*	30 (1)	30	12–43 (3)	25 (16.3)
Snailfish	*Liparidae (family)*	13–19 (9)	15 (2.2)	12–18 (4)	16 (3.2)
Poacher	*Agonidae (family)*	8–20 (19)	16 (3.5)	10–18 (4)	14 (4.3)
Sturgeon poacher	*Podothecus accipenserinus*	20 (1)	20	–	–
Daubed shanny	*Leptoclinus maculatus*	28–45 (4)	37 (6.9)	–	–
Snake prickleback	*Lumpenus sagitta*	22–67 (15)	45 (17.1)	23–47 (22)	37 (9.5)
Longsnout prickleback	*Lumpenella longirostris*	–	–	50 (1)	50
Lumpenus sp.	*Lumpenus spp.*	23 (2)	23 (0)	–	–
Larval prickleback	*Sticheaidae (Family)*	21–63 (19)	41 (15.5)	26 (1)	26
Quillfish	*Ptilichthys goodei*	–	–	173 (1)	173
Prowfish	*Zaprora silenus*	26–36 (4)	31 (4.8)	25 (1)	25
Pacific sandfish	*Trichodon trichodon*	57 (1)	57	–	–
Pacific sand lance	*Ammodytes hexapterus*	23–43 (5)	30 (7.9)	16–28 (2)	22 (8.5)
Flathead sole	*Hippoglossoides elassodon*	12–25 17)	20 (3.1)	9–38 (224)	21 (5.5)
Butter sole	*Isopsetta isolepis*	18–25 (8)	21 (2.4)	–	–
Northern rock sole	*Lepidopsetta polyxystra*	15–21 (6)	18 (2.4)	12–17 (3)	15 (2.5)
Sand sole	*Psettichthys melanosticus*	13–21 (4)	16 (3.6)	10 (1)	10
Rock Sole (unidentified)	*Lepidopsetta spp.*	13–22 (3)	16 (4.9)	–	–
Larval flatfish	*Pleuronectidae (Family)*	12–24 (23)	19 (3.5)	–	–

Table 10. Results from 3-way fixed effects permutation-based MANOVA under the null hypothesis that there was no difference in Bray Curtis similarity index of Kittlitz's murrelet zooplankton prey species in glacial versus distal stations (glacial), Aialik versus Northwestern (fjord), or time period (month).

Source	SS	MS	Pseudo-F	P
Glacial	1,517.6	1,517.6	1.3477	0.218
Fjord	2,698.3	2,698.3	2.3962	0.029
Month	8,160.7	8,160.7	7.2469	0.003
Residual	13,513	1,126.1		
Total	25,890			

Table 11. Species, size (fork length, mm), and sample size (n) of nearshore fishes captured with a beach seine in Kenai Fjords, Alaska, 2007–08.

[SD, standard deviation; n, sample size]

Common name	Scientific name	Size range (n)	Average (SD)
Pacific herring	*Clupea pallasii*	30–143 (155)	98 (20.9)
Capelin	*Mallotus villosus*	105 (1)	105
surf smelt	*Hypomesus pretiosus*	37–145 (62)	87 (32.8)
Chum salmon	*Oncorhynchus keta*	39–69 (96)	59 (7.6)
Pink salmon	*Oncorhynchus gorbuscha*	32–134 (636)	87 (21.1)
Sockeye	*Oncorhynchus nerka*	59–104 (46)	84 (12.7)
Dolly varden char	*Salvelinus malma*	150–202 (3)	184 (29.5)
Silver Salmon	*Oncorhynchus kisutch*	149 (1)	149
Pacific cod	*Gadus macrocephalus*	50–95 (86)	64 (8.3)
Threespine stickleback	*Gasterosteus aculeatus*	29 (1)	29
greenling	*Hexagrammos sp.*	28 (1)	28
Rock greenling	*Hexagrammos lagocephalus*	140 (1)	140
White-spotted greenling	*Hexagrammos stelleri*	64–82 (15)	71 (4.5)
Sculpin	*Cottidae (family)*	12–15 (2)	14 (2.1)
Padded sculpin	*Artedius fenestralis*	34 (1)	34
Buffalo sculpin	*Enophrys bison*	45–119 (7)	78 (23.0)
Great sculpin	*Myoxocephalus polyacanthocephalus*	32–159 (5)	68 (51.3)
sharpnose sculpin	*Clinocottus acuticeps*	17–27 (2)	22 (7.1)
Myox sp.	*Myoxocephalus sp.*	12–20 (21)	17 (2.3)
Eelpout	*Lycodapus sp.*	37 (1)	37
Daubed shanny	*Lumpenus maculatus*	61 (1)	61
Crescent gunnel	*Pholis laeta*	39 (1)	39
Pacific sand lance	*Ammodytes hexapterus*	32–156 (1757)	97 (33.9)
Yellowfin sole	*Pleuronectes asper*	45 (1)	45

Table 12. Parameter estimates for best-fit model using generalized linear-mixed models to relate Kittlitz's and marbled murrelet presence/absence (binomial response) to marine habitat variables measured in Kenai Fjords National Park, Alaska, July 2008.

[Acoustic backscatter was log-transformed, and all continuous variables were normalized prior to analysis to allow direct comparison of coefficients. The coefficient for fjord reflects the difference in mean probability of occurrence between fjords at the logit scale]

Kittlitz's murrelet (400-m segment lengths)				
	Coefficient	SE	t	p
Intercept	-8.7408	1.8674	-4.68	< 0.001
Bathymetry	1.7453	0.5563	3.14	< 0.01
Acoustic	1.8992	0.5461	3.48	< 0.001
Glacial Distance	-6.0131	1.3055	-4.61	< 0.001
Fjord (Aialik = 1)	6.9365	1.9259	3.6	< 0.01

Marbled murrelet (800-m segment lengths)				
	Coefficient	SE	t	p
Intercept	0.6718	0.377	1.78	0.0779
Bathymetry	-0.3268	0.2414	-1.35	0.179
Ice	-1.4687	0.5425	-2.71	< 0.01

Appendix 1. Total Count of All Birds and Marine Mammals Observed on Early Season Surveys, Kenai Fjords, Alaska, 2006–08.

[Species are arranged in taxonomic order]

Order	Family	Common name	Scientific name	Code	2006	2007	2008
Gaviiformes	Gaviidae	Common Loon	*Gavia immer*	COLO	1	6	0
		Pacific Loon	*Gavia pacifica*	PALO	0	4	0
		Red-throated Loon	*Gavia stellata*	RTLO	0	0	1
		Red-necked Grebe	*Podiceps grisegena*	RNGR	1	0	0
Pelecaniformes	Phalacrocoracidae	Double-crested Cormorant	*Phalacrocorax auritus*	DCCO	3	7	15
		Pelagic Cormorant	*Phalacrocorax pelagicus*	PECO	24	1	22
		Red-faced Cormorant	*Phalacrocorax urile*	RFCO	0	0	4
		Unidentified Cormorant	*Phalacrocorax spp.*	UNCO	5	0	2
Anseriformes	Anatidae	Mallard	*Anas platyrhychos*	MALL	16	0	0
		Harlequin Duck	*Histrionicus histrionicus*	HADU	27	30	9
		Surf scoter	*Melanitta perspicillata*	SUSC	0	0	6
		White-winged Scoter	*Melanitta fusca*	WWSC	0	51	0
		Barrow's Goldeneye	*Bucephala islandica*	BAGO	0	2	2
		Common Merganser	*Mergus merganser*	COME	4	14	0
		Red-breasted Merganser	*Mergus serrator*	RBME	0	0	1
		Greater Scaup	*Aythya marila*	GRSC	4	22	51
		Unidentified Duck		UNDU	0	4	0
Falconiformes	Accipitridae	Bald Eagle	*Haliaeetus leucocephalus*	BAEA	2	3	4

Appendix 1. Total Count of All Birds and Marine Mammals Observed on Early Season Surveys, Kenai Fjords, Alaska, 2006–08.—Continued

Order	Family	Common name	Scientific name	Code	2006	2007	2008
Charadriiformes	Haematopodidae	Black Oystercatcher	*Haematopus bachmani*	BLOY	3	1	1
	Scolopacidae	Black Turnstone	*Arenaria melanocephala*	BLTU	0	1	0
		Red-necked Phalarope	*Phalaropus lobatus*	RNPH	1	0	0
	Laridae	Parasitic Jaeger	*Stercorarius parasiticus*	PAJA	0	1	0
		Pomarine Jaeger	*Stercorarius pomarinus*	POJA	0	1	0
		Mew Gull	*Larus canus*	MEGU	9	13	7
		Glaucous-winged Gull	*Larus glaucescens*	GWGU	196	270	193
		Herring Gull	*Larus argentatus*	HEGU	1	0	0
		Black-legged Kittiwake	*Rissa tridactyla*	BLKI	10	317	27
		Arctic Tern	*Sterna paradisaea*	ARTE	12	3	1
	Alcidae	Common Murre	*Uria aalge*	COMU	0	9	0
		Pigeon Guillemot	*Cepphus columba*	PIGU	83	78	35
		marbled murrelet	*Brachyramphus marmoratus*	MAMU	236	435	102
		Kittlitz's murrelet	*Brachyramphus brevirostris*	KIMU	48	65	19
		Unidentified *Brachyramphus* murrelet	*Brachyramphus* spp.	BRMU	5	40	9
		Rhinoceros Auklet	*Cerorhinca monocerata*	RHAU	5	2	0
		Horned Puffin	*Fratercula corniculata*	HOPU	1	3	13
Passeriformes	Corvidae	Common Raven	*Corvus corax*	CORA	0	1	0
		Northwestern Crow	*Corvus caurinus*	NOCR	1	0	3
Carnivora	Mustelidae	Sea Otter	*Enhydra lutris*	SEOT	11	48	13
	Mustelidae	River Otter	*Lutra canadensis*	RIOT	0	0	1
	Otariidae	Steller Sea Lion	*Eumetopias jubatus*	STSL	3	1	0
	Phocidae	Harbor Seal	*Phoca vitulina*	HASE	45	49	13
	Urcidae	Black Bear	*Ursus americanus*	BLBE	0	0	1
Cetacea (Mysticeti)	Balaenopteridae	Humpback Whale	*Megaptera novaeangliae*	HUWH	2	0	1

Appendix 2. Total Count of All Birds and Marine Mammals Observed on Mid-Season Surveys, Kenai Fjords, Alaska, 2006–08.

[Species are arranged in taxonomic order]

Order	Family	Common name	Scientific name	Species Code	2006	2007	2008
Gaviiformes	Gaviidae	Common Loon	*Gavia immer*	COLO	1	2	1
		Unidentified Loon	*Gavia* sp.	UNLO	0	0	1
		Sooty Shearwater	*Puffinus griseus*	SOSH	1	0	0
Pelecaniformes	Phalacrocoracidae	Double-crested Cormorant	*Phalacrocorax auritus*	DCCO	238	57	155
		Red-faced Cormorant	*Phalacrocorax urile*	RFCO	25	99	219
		Pelagic Cormorant	*Phalacrocorax pelagicus*	PECO	298	135	220
		Unidentified Cormorant	*Phalacrocorax* sp.	UNCO	70	11	68
Anseriformes	Anatidae	Brant	*Branta bernicla*	BRAN	0	1	0
		Canada Goose	*Branta canadensis*	CAGO	0	1	0
		Green-winged Teal	*Anas crecca*	GRTE	0	1	0
		Harlequin Duck	*Histrionicus histrionicus*	HADU	96	100	161
		Surf Scoter	*Melanitta perspicillata*	SUSC	64	132	37
		White-winged Scoter	*Melanitta fusca*	WWSC	32	17	20
		Common Merganser	*Mergus merganser*	COME	99	31	11
		Red-breasted Merganser	*Mergus serrator*	RBME	0	5	0
Falconiformes	Accipitridae	Bald Eagle	*Haliaeetus leucocephalus*	BAEA	50	42	26

61

Appendix 2. Total Count of All Birds and Marine Mammals Observed on Mid-Season Surveys, Kenai Fjords, Alaska, 2006–08.—Continued

Order	Family	Scientific name	Common name	Species Code	2006	2007	2008
Charadriiformes	Haematopodidae	*Haematopus bachmani*	Black Oystercatcher	BLOY	13	4	15
	Scolopacidae	*Arenaria melanocephala*	Black Turnstone	BLTU	0	0	1
	Laridae	*Phalaropus fulicaria*	Red Phalarope	RNPH	0	0	11
		Larus canus	Mew Gull	MEGU	45	6	17
		Larus glaucescens	Glaucous-winged Gull	GWGU	4,751	1,208	3,106
		Larus argentatus	Herring Gull	HEGU	6	0	1
		Rissa tridactyla	Black-legged Kittiwake	BLKI	1,126	497	480
	Alcidae	*Uria aalge*	Common Murre	COMU	162	138	22
		Uria sp.	Unidentified Murre	UNMU	0	3	0
		Cepphus columba	Pigeon Guillemot	PIGU	292	266	287
		Synthiliboramphus antiquus	Ancient murrelet	ANMU	2	0	0
		Brachyramphus marmoratus	marbled murrelet	MAMU	857	493	1,277
		Brachyramphus brevirostris	Kittlitz's murrelet	KIMU	81	37	69
		Brachyramphus sp.	Unidentified *Brachyramphus* murrelet	BRMU	27	37	192
		Cerorhinca monocerata	Rhinoceros Auklet	RHAU	262	5	172
		Fratercula corniculata	Horned Puffin	HOPU	397	154	449
		Fratercula cirrhata	Tufted Puffin	TUPU	214	157	151
Passeriformes	Corvidae	*Corvus caurinus*	Northwestern Crow	NOCR	0	35	7
Carnivora	Mustelidae	*Enhydra lutris*	Sea Otter	SEOT	123	71	185
	Mustelidae	*Lutra canadensis*	River Otter	RIOT	0	1	1
	Otariidae	*Eumetopias jubatus*	Steller Sea Lion	STSL	33	12	3
	Phocidae	*Phoca vitulina*	Harbor Seal	HASE	146	88	103
	Urcidae	*Ursus Americanus*	Black Bear	BLBE	1	0	1
Cetacea (Mysticeti)	Balaenopteridae	*Megaptera novaeangliae*	Humpback Whale	HUWH	1	1	2
Cetacea (Odontoceti)	Phocoenidae	*Phocoenoides dalli*	Dall's Porpoise	DAPO	0	1	1

Appendix 3. Total Count of Birds and Marine Mammals Observed on Late-Season Surveys, Kenai Fjords, Alaska, 2006–08.

[Species are arranged in taxonomic order]

Order	Family	Scientific name	Common name	Species	2006	2007	2008
Pelecaniformes	Phalacrocoracidae	Phalacrocorax auritus	Double-crested Cormorant	DCCO	18	53	27
		Phalacrocorax pelagicus	Pelagic Cormorant	PECO	9	8	3
		Phalacrocorax urile	Red-faced Cormorant	RFCO	1	0	1
		Phalacrocorax spp.	Unidentified Cormorant	UNCO	0	1	3
Anseriformes	Anatidae	Histrionicus histrionicus	Harlequin Duck	HADU	51	108	7
		Anas platyrhynchos	Mallard	MALL	3	0	0
		Melanitta perspicillata	Surf Scoter	SUSC	12	2	16
		Melanitta fusca	White-winged Scoter	WWSC	0	10	0
		Melanitta spp.	Unidentified Scoter	UNSC	0	7	0
		Mergus serrator	Red_breasted Merganser	RBME	35	0	0
		Mergus merganser	Common Merganser	COME	0	28	39
			Unidentified Duck	UNDU	0	2	0
Falconiformes	Accipitridae	Haliaeetus leucocephalus	Bald Eagle	BAEA	2	9	0
Charadriiformes	Haematopodidae	Haematopus bachmani	Black Oystercatcher	BLOY	3	0	15
	Scolopacidae	Arenaria melanocephala	Black Turnstone	BLTU	0	1	0
		Phalaropus lobatus	Red-necked Phalarope	RNPH	0	71	25

Appendix 3. Total Count of Birds and Marine Mammals Observed on Late-Season Surveys, Kenai Fjords, Alaska, 2006–08.—Continued

Order	Family	Scientific name	Common name	Species	2006	2007	2008
Charadriiformes	Laridae	*Stercorarius pomarinus*	Pomarine Jaeger	POJA	0	2	0
		Larus canus	Mew Gull	MEGU	1	7	3
		Larus glaucescens	Glaucous-winged Gull	GWGU	295	1,183	800
		Rissa tridactyla	Black-legged Kittiwake	BLKI	121	258	130
		Sterna paradisaea	Arctic Tern	ARTE	5	2	0
	Alcidae	*Uria aalge*	Common Murre	COMU	52	31	48
		Uria lomvia	Thick-billed Murre	TBMU	0	1	0
		Cepphus columba	Pigeon Guillemot	PIGU	30	100	48
		Synthliboramphus antiquus	Ancient murrelet	ANMU	0	0	6
		Brachyramphus marmoratus	marbled murrelet	MAMU	345	1,120	306
		Brachyramphus brevirostris	Kittlitz's murrelet	KIMU	13	43	14
		Brachyramphus spp.	Unidentified *Brachyramphus* murrelet	BRMU	17	71	28
		Cerorhinca monocerata	Rhinoceros Auklet	RHAU	30	485	29
		Fratercula corniculata	Horned Puffin	HOPU	20	54	165
		Fratercula cirrhata	Tufted Puffin	TUPU	45	40	164
Passeriformes	Corvidae	*Corvus caurinus*	Northwestern Crow	NOCR	0	8	0
Carnivora	Mustelidae	*Enhydra lutris*	Sea Otter	SEOT	19	8	37
	Phocidae	*Phoca vitulina*	Harbor Seal	HASE	225	65	30
	Urcidae	*Ursus americanus*	Black Bear	BLBE	0	1	0
Cetacea (Mysticeti)	Balaenopteridae	*Megaptera novaeangliae*	Humpback Whale	HUWH	0	0	1

Appendix 4. Catch Per Unit Effort (CPUE, # m-3) and Frequency of Occurrence (FO) of Small Zooplankton at Stations Sampled with a Ring Net, Kenai Fjords, Alaska, 2007.

[Species are arranged in order of relative abundance. Sample size, 21; SD, standard deviation]

Taxon	Species	Mean CPUE	SD	FO
Copepod	*Pseudocalanus* spp.	25,741.64	15,582.57	1
Copepod	*Oithona similis*	6,363.39	274.79	1
Copepod	*Acartia longiremis*	27,28.71	2,597.47	1
Copepod	*Calanus marshallae*	161.26	187.96	1
Chaetognath	*Sagitta elegans*	69.82	67.26	1
Gastropod	*Limacina helicina*	22.48	241.12	1
Gastropod	Gastropod larvae	233.66	488.64	0.96
Larvacean	*Oikopleura* sp.	14.83	97.84	0.96
Copepod	*Metridia pacifica*	128.27	125.35	0.92
Copepod	*Centropages abdominalis*	81.33	8.55	0.88
Copepod	*Eucalanus bungii*	25.94	27.75	0.79
Decapod	Hippolytidae zoea	3.38	3.97	0.75
Bivalve	Bivalvia	135.22	277.17	0.71
Euphausiid	Euphausiid (nauplii-juvenile)	8.19	12.94	0.71
Copepod	*Neocalanus flemingeri*	4.25	5.14	0.71
Decapod	Paguridae zoea	2.52	2.86	0.71
Cladoceran	Evadnae	286.52	147.25	0.58
Hydrozoan	*Bougainvilla* sp	0.34	0.47	0.5
Copepod	*Neocalanus plumchrus*	1.72	2.54	0.46
Copepod	Copepoda nauplii	251.86	685.72	0.42
Decapod	Pisinae zoea	1.23	2.14	0.42
Decapod	Brachyrhancha zoea	2.78	6.29	0.29
Decapod	Pinnotheridae zoea	0.47	1.22	0.29
Copepod	Oncea	36.29	89.55	0.25
Cnidarian	*Aglantha digitale*	0.28	0.62	0.25
Barnacle	Cirripedia	23.9	76.86	0.21
Polychaete	Polychaete	10	32.51	0.21
Copepod	Harpacticoida	7.34	27.71	0.21
Cnidarian	Anthomedusae	2.85	7.19	0.21
Cnidarian	*Coryne princeps*	0.3	0.79	0.21
Copepod	*Neocalanus cristatus*	0.18	0.47	0.21
Cnidarian	Leptomedusae	0.11	0.28	0.21
Nemertea	Nemertina	6.16	27.67	0.17
Isopod	Cryptoniscidae	2.66	7.17	0.17
Amphipod	*Parathemisto* sp.	0.89	2.89	0.17
Decapod	*Pandalus* sp.	0.61	0.14	0.17
Decapod	Pandalidae zoea	0.46	1.44	0.17
Gastropod	*Clione limacina*	0.24	0.76	0.17
Copepod	*Microcalanus* sp.	11.17	42.5	0.13
Mysiid	Mysidacea	0.62	0.23	0.08
Copepod	*Epilabedocera amphitrites*	0.41	1.41	0.08

Appendix 4. Catch Per Unit Effort (CPUE, # m-3) and Frequency of Occurrence (FO) of Small Zooplankton at Stations Sampled with a Ring Net, Kenai Fjords, Alaska, 2007.—Continued

Taxon	Species	Mean CPUE	SD	FO
Cnidarian	Rathkea	0.23	0.81	0.08
Hydrozoan	*Lars flavicirratus*	0.12	0.44	0.08
Copepod	*Scolethricella minor*	4.53	22.17	0.04
Copepod	*Oithona spinirostra*	1.13	5.54	0.04
Euphausiid	*Thysanoessa raschii*	0.88	0.43	0.04
Amphipod	*Parathemisto libellula*	0.88	0.43	0.04
Cladocrean	Podon	0.47	2.4	0.04
Gastropod	Echinospira	0.47	2.4	0.04
Copepod	*Calanus pacificus*	0.35	1.73	0.04
Decapod	Oregoninae zoea	0.35	0.17	0.04
Polychaete	Syllidae	0.35	0.17	0.04
Decapod	Crangonidae zoea	0.22	0.18	0.04
Ostracod	*Conchoceia* sp.	0.18	0.87	0.04
Euphausiid	*Euphausia pacifica*	0.18	0.87	0.04
Siphonophore	Siphonophore Bract	0.18	0.87	0.04

Appendix 5. Catch Per Unit Effort (CPUE, # m-3) and Frequency of Occurrence (FO) of Small Zooplankton at Stations Sampled with a Ring Net, Kenai Fjords, Alaska, 2008.

[Species are arranged in order of relative abundance. Sample size, 24. SD, standard deviation]

Taxon	Species	Mean CPUE	SD	FO
Copepod	*Pseudocalanus* spp.	128,853.33	73,987.36	1.00
Copepod	*Oithona similis*	35,232.00	16,493.34	1.00
Copepod	*Acartia longiremis*	16,586.67	12,195.59	0.96
Euphausiid	Euphausiid (nauplii-juvenile)	1,937.42	2,855.71	0.96
Copepod	*Calanus marshallae*	692.83	1,051.33	0.96
Chaetognath	*Sagitta elegans*	284.46	343.62	0.92
Gastropod	*Limacina helicina*	900.83	1,212.42	0.83
Copepod	*Eucalanus bungii*	60.50	114.67	0.79
Copepod	*Metridia pacifica*	1,258.67	1,568.50	0.75
Gastropod	Gastropod larvae	1,074.67	1,198.22	0.75
Larvacean	*Oikopleura* sp.	825.33	1,033.35	0.71
Copepod	*Neocalanus plumchrus*	421.50	763.74	0.67
Copepod	Copepoda nauplii	3,424.00	4,937.44	0.63
Copepod	*Centropages abdominalis*	371.33	838.52	0.58
Decapod	Hippolytidae zoea	10.50	16.29	0.54
Bivalve	Bivalvia	1,241.33	2,842.61	0.46
Polychaete	Polychaete	433.33	726.04	0.46
Amphipod	*Parathemisto* sp.	15.17	28.75	0.46
Barnacle	Cirripedia	321.33	482.50	0.42
Gastropod	Echinospira	233.33	668.41	0.38
Cnidarian	*Eirene indicans*	6.04	14.53	0.33
Cladoceran	Evadnae	234.00	671.57	0.29
Decapod	Paguridae zoea	4.33	8.74	0.29
Cnidarian	*Aglantha digitale*	4.00	10.20	0.29
Cladoceran	Podon	19.33	47.88	0.21
Decapod	Pisinae zoea	2.83	7.69	0.17
Decapod	Brachyrhancha zoea	2.00	6.67	0.17
Larvacean	*Fritillaria* sp.	192.00	581.08	0.13
Echinoderm	Echinodermata	108.00	426.18	0.13
Isopod	Cryptoniscidae	106.67	301.17	0.13
Copepod	*Neocalanus flemingeri*	8.42	39.14	0.13
Cnidarian	*Coryne princeps*	0.54	1.79	0.13
Copepod	*Epilabedocera amphitrites*	0.25	0.68	0.13
Copepod	Harpacticoida	86.67	417.81	0.08
Copepod	Oncea	24.00	104.76	0.08
Bryzoan	Bryozoa cyphonautes	24.00	104.76	0.08
Copepod	*Acartia tumida*	6.67	26.66	0.08

Appendix 5. Catch Per Unit Effort (CPUE, # m-3) and Frequency of Occurrence (FO) of Small Zooplankton at Stations Sampled with a Ring Net, Kenai Fjords, Alaska, 2008.—Continued

Taxon	Species	Mean CPUE	SD	FO
Cnidarian	Rathkea	6.33	26.37	0.08
Hydrozoan	*Bougainvilla* sp	1.17	4.93	0.08
Copepod	*Neocalanus cristatus*	0.50	1.79	0.08
Amphipod	*Cyphocaris challengeri*	0.38	1.64	0.08
Cnidarian	*Perigonimus* sp.	0.38	1.64	0.08
Echinoderm	Echinodermata "pleutes"	42.67	209.02	0.04
Copepod	*Oithona spinirostra*	2.67	13.06	0.04
Copepod	*Metridia ochatensis*	1.83	8.98	0.04
Fish	Fish (sm)	1.00	4.90	0.04
Copepod	*Calanus pacificus*	0.33	1.63	0.04
Fish	Plueronectidae	0.33	1.63	0.04
Amphipod	*Parathemisto libellula*	0.25	1.22	0.04
Decapod	*Pandalus platyceros*	0.17	0.82	0.04
Decapod	Oregoninae zoea	0.17	0.82	0.04
Amphipod	*Hyperoche meduserum*	0.08	0.41	0.04
Hydrozoan	*Lars flavicirratus*	0.08	0.41	0.04
Decapod	*Pandalopsis dispar*	0.04	0.20	0.04
Euphausiid	*Thysanoessa inremis*	0.04	0.20	0.04
Euphausiid	*Euphausia pacifica*	0.04	0.20	0.04